MODERN
JAPANESE
PRINTS

Frontispiece (see over):
Impression of a Violinist
by KOSHIRO ONCHI

Reproduced by newly carved blocks
through the kindness of
THE ADACHI INSTITUTE OF WOODCUT PRINTS

MODERN JAPANESE PRINTS + AN ART REBORN

by
OLIVER STATLER

with an introduction by
JAMES A. MICHENER

CHARLES E. TUTTLE COMPANY
RUTLAND, VERMONT
TOKYO, JAPAN

European Representatives
Continent: Boxerbooks, Inc., Zurich
British Isles: Prentice-Hall International Inc., London

Published by
Charles E. Tuttle Company
Rutland, Vermont & Tokyo, Japan
with editorial offices at
15 Edogawa-cho, Bunkyo-ku, Tokyo

Library of Congress
Catalog Card No. 56–6810

First printing, 1956
Seventh printing, 1963

Book design & typography
by M. Weatherby

Printed in Japan

TO THE MEMORY OF

KOSHIRO
ONCHI

Koshiro Onchi
by Jun'ichiro Sekino

CONTENTS

CONTENTS

ILLUSTRATIONS

xii

INTRODUCTION

The publication of this book could not come at a better time. In the natural course of historical events, Japan is temporarily drawing away from the orbit of American influence. This is both inevitable and healthy, for a Japan which supinely hid behind American leadership would in the long run prove to be a very weak friend indeed.

But in such uncertain and difficult times it is good to have a book like this appear to remind us all that American interest in Japanese culture is not only permanent but occasionally profound.

This book is a work of love. It is an account of modern Japanese creative prints written by a man who under his own initiative has studied the art and championed the artists. There is no Japanese woodblock artist working today who does not know and revere Oliver Statler, a quiet American who entered Japan as a civilian employee of the army during the first years of the Occupation, and ended as a private citizen dedicated to scholarship.

Mr. Statler has personally collected what is probably the world's finest collection of modern Japanese creative prints. He has personally arranged for the sale of hundreds of other prints to museums throughout the United States. He has taken dozens of American tourists to the workshops of Tokyo woodblock artists and has acted as intermediary in literally hundreds of sales. He has mailed Japanese prints on approval to many private citizens in the United States.

And he has performed all these services without accepting a penny or a yen of commission. He is the best friend a group of living artists ever had.

As a scholar, Mr. Statler probably knows more about modern Japanese prints than anyone not a Japanese, and possibly more than any Japanese other than experts like Un'ichi Hiratsuka, Shizuya Fujikake, and Toyohisa Adachi. He has studied intimately with at least eight of the artists represented in this book and has closely followed the work of all the others.

He therefore becomes yet another American in the long history of modern Japan who has immersed himself in the culture of the Japanese islands. Ernest Fenollosa was the first American, and almost the first human being, to awaken the world to the scholarly problems relating to Japanese prints. Louis Ledoux was merely the last in a long line of experts who taught the West to appreciate the beauties of classical Japanese prints. After the war, William Hartnett, a soldier-civilian like Mr. Statler, pioneered in the discovery of contemporary Japanese prints.

This interests me a great deal, because I travel much in Asia and am constantly being told that Americans cannot appreciate either the art or the spirit of another land. Yet while the men named were studying Japanese prints, other Americans were among the first to recognize the merit of modern French painting, so that today, just as the finest collections of Japanese prints are in the United States, whose scholars early realized the merit of this art, so the finest assemblies of modern French painting are also in the United States, where men like Renoir, Manet, and Cezanne were almost immediately recognized as great artists.

I would not want to compare Jun'ichiro Sekino or Kiyoshi Saito with the great French moderns. I am not qualified to say how good Munakata and Hiratsuka are in comparison with artists of the last century. But I do know that at least a dozen of the living men discussed in this book are very wonderful artists.

I can attest to the tremendous effectiveness of their work. I have shown their prints in several American cities and have listened to the remarks of observers who saw for the first time the dazzling work being done in contemporary Japan. I find in it a power, a mastery of color, and a variety that make it the equal of any other graphic work being done in the world today.

For example, one who studies the illustrations contained in this book would find great difficulty in identifying more than half the prints as Japanese. This is good. It means that the artsts who did these prints had outgrown the trivial job of creating pretty little tourist postcards showing Mount Fuji and geisha girls. These artists are in the full world stream of art.

Yet, at the same time, some of the most immediately appealing prints contained in this book are those which clearly bespeak their Japanese heritage. This also is good. It means the artists who did these particular prints were not afraid to go to purely Japanese subject matter for their inspiration. Although part of the great world stream of art, they remained Japanese.

What pleases me most is that, in almost every instance, the same artist is able to do both international prints, whose subject matter is universal, and emphatically Japanese subjects, whose spirit is unmistakably Japanese. This is maturity. This proves that modern Japanese creative prints can be judged by world standards of great art, rather than as tourist art to be sold to Westerners who want some "Japanesey trinkets" to take home.

But this book is not only an excellent introduction, well illustrated, to modern Japanese prints; it is also a loving record of the artists who have created this beauty. Suppose Mr. Statler had not studied so hard in order to explain how Koshiro Onchi worked? Now that Onchi is dead, where could we have looked for the faithful reporting contained in this record? I am positively convinced that in decades to come our descendants will prize the work of Saito and Sekino, to name but two, in the way we prize the prints of Kiyonaga and Utamaro. It seems to me inconceivable that their work could remain unrecognized.

In that day how fortunate the scholars will be to have before them this record of how Azechi became an artist, how Shinagawa feels for form, how great Onchi burst the shackles of an art and set whole families of artists free. In fact, if Mr. Statler had done nothing but assemble from old memories the account of Kanae Yamamoto, the founder of the school, he would have earned our gratitude. That he has done so much more makes it a pleasure for me to commend his book to the public, both American and Japanese.

JAMES A. MICHENER

PREFACE

From the time they first laid eyes on them, foreigners have been captivated by Japanese prints. Toward the end of the last century, the *ukiyoe* of the Edo period (1615–1867) cut a wide swath through Europe and America, and the excitement they engendered then still lingers. A growing number of foreigners are finding something of the same excitement today as they seek out the great prints of contemporary Japanese artists.

This book is concerned only with *sosaku hanga,* the creative prints which are one-man works. It cannot cover all the artists, for there are more than three hundred working in the media of *sosaku hanga* today. My aim has been a representative and diversified selection, but such a choice is necessarily controversial and I shall be delighted if controversy ensues. My hope is that the reader will seek out the prints of the movement—for they are now to be found all over the world—and decide for himself.

With the exception of the great pioneer, Yamamoto, and the great realizer, Onchi, whose death midway in the preparation of this book saddened the whole effort, attention is confined to artists who are actively working today. I have tried to tell something of their lives and their thinking, of the way they work and the background of their prints, but I have not attempted a critical analysis of their art, because I feel that the prints speak for themselves.

There is a woeful lack of material on this subject in English. James A. Michener has provided a brilliant introduction in the last chapter of *The Floating World,* telling the story in terms of but two artists, Koshiro Onchi and Un'ichi Hiratsuka. The only other comprehensive reference in English is Dr. Shizuya Fujikake's invaluable handbook, *Japanese Wood-block Prints,* published in the Japan Travel Bureau's Tourist Library. Because of the limited material available, I have tried to avoid reproducing prints already shown in either of these two books, but in some cases an important print demanded inclusion.

I cannot list here all those who helped me, but I must acknowledge the helpful suggestions made by Ellen Psaty and the kind assistance of Professors Joseph Roggendorf, S. J., and Edward G. Seidensticker, who translated the poems of Koshiro Onchi which appear in the appendix. And I am especially grateful to Ansei Uchima, who saw me through my language difficulties. The fact that Uchima is also an artist made everything easier, and one of the pleasantest rewards of this work has been entirely unexpected: Uchima himself has turned to the medium of prints with every indication of brilliant success. He does not belong in this book, because he is an American, but his prints show again what happy results can come from cross-fertilization in art.

This book would be incomplete without mention of William Hartnett. I, and many more like me, first saw modern Japanese prints through the exhibitions he arranged in the early days of the Occupation. Hartnett's taste and enthusiasm played an enormous part in giving these artists the encouragement and recognition they needed, and for his good work we may all be grateful.

The frontispiece is the gift of Toyohisa Adachi, one of the notable publishers of prints in Japan today. In producing this woodblock reproduction of Koshiro Onchi's *Impression of a Violinist,* Adachi drew on the finest skills available, and the result is faithful even in spirit. His gift is not only a warm act of friendship but a generous tribute to the work of Onchi and the *sosaku* artists.

Both general and technical information concerning the prints reproduced in the book will be found in an appendix. Also given in an appendix is brief data on the woods used by contemporary Japanese artsts to make the blocks for their prints.

Paper is obviously of vital importance in print-making, but the subject is an extremely technical one. Prints are invariably made on handmade papers (to the Japanese these are "Japanese" papers; machine-made papers are "Western" papers). The fibers of most of the handmade papers of Japan come from the inner bark of one of three plants. *Gampi (Wickstroemia shikokiana,* Franchet et Savatier) papers are tough, lustrous, and long-lived, but non-absorbent and therefore little used for prints. *Mitsumata (Edgeworthia papyrifera,*

Siebold et Zuccarini) is of the same family as *gampi* but more refined; mixed with pulp it is used to make modern *torinoko,* a paper which is very popular among the *sosaku hanga* artists (the frontispiece is made on a *torinoko* paper). *Kozo* (*Broussonetia kazinoki,* Siebold) is of the same family as mulberry; its fibers are sinewy and tough, with an appealing roughness; *kozo* papers are strong, elastic, and porous, and are widely used in print-making. Japanese writers have ascribed noble dignity to *gampi* papers, gentle elegance to *mitsumata* papers, and tough masculinity to *kozo* papers, but the print artist is less concerned with these poetic attributes than he is with practical considerations such as absorbency, strength, and color reaction.

Japanese names are given throughout in the foreign manner, that is, with the given name first and the family name last. For those who are interested, in the index the long vowels of Japanese words have been indicated and, in the case of names, Japanese characters added.

And finally, though this is by no means a technical treatise, a few Japanese words relating to the technique of the woodblock reoccur, and definition here may simplify things. They are:

Baren: the pad, faced with a bamboo sheath, with which the printer rubs the back of his paper as it lies on the printing block in order to fix the impression on the paper.

Kento: the marks on the corners of a printing block by which the printer positions his paper on the block to insure registry.

Sumi: the black ink which the Japanese use for painting, for writing with a brush, and, of course, for making prints.

OLIVER STATLER

Tokyo, February 15, 1956

ACKNOWLEDGMENTS

The quotation from James A. Michener's *The Floating World* is used by permission of Random House, New York; the quotation from Langdon Warner's *The Enduring Art of Japan,* by permission of the Harvard University Press, Cambridge; and the quotation from Elise Grilli's review of the work of Koshiro Onchi, by permission of the writer.

The present work had its genesis in a paper read before the Asiatic Society of Japan on February 14, 1955, a revised version of which was published in Sophia University's quarterly, *Monumenta Nipponica,* July, 1955. Grateful acknowledgment is made to both the Society and the University for the cooperation which helped to make this publication possible.

MODERN
JAPANESE
PRINTS

I
AN ART
REBORN

"ART MUST MOVE IN CYCLES. THERE MUST BE CONTINUOUS INTER-change. The new must become old and die. The old must come back...."

With these words James A. Michener closes *The Floating World,* the trenchant and illuminating book in which he pictures the life and death of the traditional art of *ukiyoe,* the great woodblock prints of Japan. As we look back at the history of *ukiyoe,* its inglorious death is as evident as its magnificent life, and yet, because art does move in cycles, Michener was able to end on a note of optimism as he described the rebirth of prints today.

For Japanese prints have been reborn. Revived is not the proper word. You will look in vain for modern prints of beautiful women like Utamaro's, of actors like Sharaku's, or of landscapes like Hiro-shige's. What we are experiencing is a renascence, not a restoration. The new prints are as much a part of today as old *ukiyoe* prints were of their day. And it does not take a historian to grasp the difference between the Japan of today—industrial, centralized,

3

inextricably caught up in international currents—and the Japan of *ukiyoe*'s day—agricultural, feudal, sealed from the outside world, an introverted recluse.

This is no place to dwell on the death of *ukiyoe*. The era of the Emperor Meiji (1868–1912), ushered in by Perry's knock on the door, saw Japan look about, take stock, and then plunge headlong into the modern world. In the upheaval there were many casualties; *ukiyoe,* already weakened by the factors Michener describes so well, was only one of these.

In their race to catch up with the Western world the Japanese made few reservations. In art, as in industry, they set out to learn new ways, and hundreds of artists turned from brushing ink on paper to daubing oil on canvas. Then some of them made an astonishing discovery. They found that their European idols, the impressionists and postimpressionists, had been obviously excited and just as obviously influenced by Japanese *ukiyoe.* It was a curious experience, to go halfway around the world to find the honored oil painters of the West in turn honoring the prints of Japan, things the Japanese themselves had never taken very seriously. Japanese artists who went to Europe made a further discovery: European artists were making their own prints—carving their own blocks, doing their own printing. It was cause for reflection.

Reflect they did, these new foreign-style artists of Japan. They reconsidered the past glories of *ukiyoe* and discerned the greatness there. They weighed the Japanese prints of their own day and saw the humiliating fall from grace. Especially, they pondered the new concept that an artist should make his own prints.

This was an idea which violated the whole tradition of *ukiyoe.* *Ukiyoe* were the astounding result of collaboration unheard of in other fields of art anywhere in the world, a collaboration between a man who provided the picture or design, a man who cut that design onto the blocks, a man who printed from those blocks, and a man who, we may suspect, was in many cases the dominant personality: the publisher. When the new print artists of Japan turned to one-man creations their self-designed, self-carved, self-printed, and mostly self-published prints were such a departure from

4

Japanese tradition that a new name was coined for them. The artists called them "creative prints."

Of course, certain woodcut prints are still being made in Japan by the time-honored artist-artisan-publisher teams. Some of these "modern *ukiyoe*" have a great deal of charm and they are backed by centuries of accumulated skill. They are a respectable reflection of a great art, but they differ significantly from traditional *ukiyoe* in at least one way. In the palmy days of *ukiyoe* the print was created in cooperative team effort. The artist's contributions were rough sketches, often uncolored, and ideally, supervision of the artisans at every vital stage of the carving and printing. For example, the original brush stroke of the *ukiyoe* artist was very different from the final print line: by common agreement the artisan did not reproduce the artist's line but carved a line based on the heart of the artist's brush stroke. "Modern *ukiyoe*" prints, however, are originally done as full-scale color paintings, by say Hasui Kawase or Shinsui Ito, which the artisans then transform into woodprints as faithfully as possible. Thus the charge that woodprints are merely a reproductive art, which is unfair when applied to the great traditional *ukiyoe*, can be leveled against those "modern *ukiyoe*" prints of today with a good deal of justification.

However, despite the fact that the *ukiyoe* tradition has been kept alive, it is impossible to trace any direct connection from the dying *ukiyoe* to the new creative prints. The connection is by rebound from the West, and the creative prints are the result of interaction between Japanese and Western influences, which continues to this day. To borrow the euphemistic phrase which the Japanese apply to their Occupation babies, modern Japanese creative prints are children of mixed blood.

On the Japanese side of this inheritance is the great technique of the woodblock print. Without this, these creative prints could never have happened. Only in Japan does any significant number of artists feel impelled to concentrate on this medium. Regardless of an artist's personal reaction to *ukiyoe*, the woodcut as a medium is deep in his national heritage.

From the West comes their artistic content, a legacy already

5

influenced by *ukiyoe*. No one is asked to believe that Japanese art does not in some degree influence a Japanese artist, but artistically most of the new prints are as Western as shoes.

The Japanese artist even dallied a while with the European style of woodcuts made from blocks cut across the grain, but speedily reverted to blocks cut along the grain in traditional *ukiyoe* style. As can be seen from the accompanying sketch, blocks cut across the grain are restricted in size to the rectangle which can be cut within the circumference of the trunk, while a block cut along the grain can be as wide as the full diameter of the trunk and, within reason, as long as the artist wishes. Furthermore, the use of the long grain of the wood

BLOCK CUT
ACROSS THE GRAIN

BLOCK CUT
ALONG THE GRAIN

as an element of the design was an inherent feature of the medium and too much in the Japanese tradition to be cast aside. Now only a handful of Japanese artists ever carve a block cut across the grain, a process they call wood engraving: Un'ichi Hiratsuka and Jun'ichiro Sekino, for example, sometimes use this technique to make book illustrations, as Thomas Bewick did in England. Today the whole problem seems a little dated, for the advent of plywood veneer has made possible larger (and cheaper, and easier to work) blocks than ever before, and most of the creative-print artists use plywood for their blocks.

From its beginnings in the first decade of this century the new creative-print movement rapidly gained momentum, and though the rest of the Japanese art world chose to ignore it, it began to attract serious attention abroad. In the 1930's a number of full-scale exhibitions went to Europe and America, but of course World War II put an end to that.

After the war the artists began the battle to re-establish themselves. In one way the fight was easier, for now the country was flooded with foreigners, and foreigners have always been the most enthusiastic champions of Japanese prints. Anyone who wonders why this is true must realize that traditional *ukiyoe* was a "popular art." It was mass-produced to sell. To sell it had to catch the public fancy—and it did, blazoning the celebrated figures and foibles of its day. It was cheap and democratic. Such a "popular ,art" always carries a stigma in its own country. Foreigners, untroubled by background associations, see it fresh and on its own merits, but it is only natural that many art-conscious Japanese, intensely proud of their nation's painting and sculpture, should regard *ukiyoe* as something on the outer fringe of artistic respectability.

Since *"ukiyoe"* and "prints" are popularly synonymous in Japan, the whole medium falls under the same shadow. And if the towering achievements of traditional *ukiyoe* are regarded with scepticism, so much the worse for a group of modern mavericks who perversely choose the same medium. Here is the ironic twist, for creative prints are not a "popular art" at all. Behind these new prints there is an entirely different urge—the conscious desire of an artist to create a work of art. The creative-print artist uses the technique of the woodprint not as a means to achieve multiple copies of a picture but as a means to create a picture.

This is the answer to the inevitable question: why do these modern artists feel it necessary to carve their own blocks when artisans might have more skill with a chisel, and to print their own pictures when other artisans might do a cleaner job?

The creative-print artist really creates his picture as he works with his wood, his chisels, and his colors. The method varies with each artist and often from print to print. He may work from a fairly complete sketch, a rough sketch, or no sketch at all, but the real act of design starts when he goes to work with block and knife, guided by his inner conception, and with full appreciation for the personality of his materials and his tools. This is a process of creation which he feels he cannot delegate.

There is another difference between traditional *ukiyoe* and modern creative prints which should be pointed out: the creative prints are not exclusively woodcuts. The Japanese have a generic term, *hanga,* which is defined as a picture made with a block. By Japanese usage this definition includes etchings, lithographs, mimeographs, and

7

similar forms as well as woodblock prints. Furthermore, in making what we commonly call woodblock prints the new artists do not restrict themselves to wood, but also use a variety of materials such as paper, string, and leaves. The creative-print artists prefer to think of their field as *hanga,* broadly defined, and many of them roam freely among the different techniques.

One of the most encouraging things about the new prints is that each artist is unique. Traditional *ukiyoe* artists usually developed in schools, the style of whose members became additionally similar because they used the same artisans. Today each of the creative artists follows his own path. The result is so lively and vigorous that it is sometimes a little difficult to keep up with developments.

In telling the story of creative prints one cannot avoid emphasizing the difficulties which these artists have had in their own country. Still there have been important exceptions, and one great expert like Shizuya Fujikake, who was the first to write critically of creative prints, goes far to balance the scale. It is worth remembering that there were a few, like this brilliant and beloved dean of *ukiyoe* scholars, who saw the strong beauty of creative prints before foreigners pointed it out. Dr. Fujikake has never wavered. "Creative *hanga* is postwar Japan's best contribution to the art of the world," he says today. "Generally speaking, Japan's postwar art is not good; the shining exception is creative *hanga.* Creative *hanga* is showing the world the good art of contemporary Japan in the same way that traditional *ukiyoe* showed the good art of an older age."

2
KANAE
YAMAMOTO

IN THE EARLY DAYS OF THE CREATIVE-PRINT movement, one figure, Kanae Yamamoto (1882–1946), looms above all the others. He produced not only Japan's first creative prints, but prints whose stature gave the whole movement a solid foundation, and even today look fresh and vital. They have none of the quaintness or mustiness that so often marks pioneer work, and on exhibition they can stand without protestation of historical importance.

Yamamoto's story properly starts with his grandfather, an attendant to the last of the Tokugawa shoguns, that long line of dictators who ruled Japan from 1603 to 1867 and effectively sealed the country against foreign intercourse for most of that period. It was a regime already weakened by dry rot when

9

Commodore Perry's bold challenge shook it, and within a few years the powerful southwestern clans, rallying under the name of the emperor, toppled it and set up a new government.

Since Yamamoto's grandfather fought on the side of the Tokugawas when they went down to final defeat, he thereafter found himself on the outside looking in, and with the country in the hands of a new and revolutionary regime he found it difficult to support his family and raise his three sons. Financial difficulty was probably one of the reasons why Kanae's father, one of those three sons, was adopted into the Yamamoto family to assume their name and marry their daughter, although this is a common enough arrangement in Japan. The Yamamotos were a long line of doctors and their new son set out to follow the family profession. He went to Shinshu (now Nagano Prefecture), in the mountainous area of central Japan, to learn medicine as an assistant to Dr. Ogai Mori, a physician who attained fame as an author.

While Kanae was a baby his mother lived with her parents in Okazaki but when he was five she moved to Tokyo to be a little closer to Shinshu. The boy was still young when his father died and his mother had to turn to housework to drudge out a living. Kanae went through elementary school but that was all the thin family-purse would allow, and at eleven, perhaps by chance, but if so very lucky chance, he was apprenticed to an illustrator and wood engraver. So he learned, not the technique of Japanese *ukiyoe,* but that of Western wood engraving. The two are diametrically opposed, not only with regard to the block (cut along the grain for *ukiyoe* and across the grain for wood engraving, as already explained), but also in the carving. In *ukiyoe* the method is by black lines on white paper, achieved by cutting away the block on both sides of the line, leaving the line to print. But in wood engraving the artist works with white lines against an area of black ink, and the method is to carve out the line itself so that it will show white against the surrounding black.

The resulting blocks are amazingly disparate in yet another way: an *ukiyoe* block, properly carved and cared for, is good for about one thousand clean impressions, in five hand-printings of two hundred each, with time between to let the blocks dry out; but the little wood-engraving block, with its fine lines delicately engraved on the end of the grain, can be put in a printing press for two hundred thousand impressions, easily outlasting a photoengraved copper plate. Photoengraving had other advantages which were soon to make it supreme, but when Yamamoto was a boy there was still a great market for the skill of the wood engraver, as one can see by a glance at the copiously illustrated books and magazines of that day. He was an apt pupil, and by the time he had finished his apprenticeship and the obligatory year which followed, he was able to get a good job.

He went to work as a wood engraver and illustrator for the forerunner of the present Yomiuri newspapers, and then at twenty-one, not wanting to remain a technician all his life, he entered the government art academy at Ueno in Tokyo. While going through art school he continued to support himself by his wood engraving. He graduated in 1906, a promising young artist.

Concerning this period, the reminiscences of Tsuruzo Ishii (born 1887) make delightful listening. A man of amazing versatility, Ishii is an oil painter, Japanese water-colorist, sculptor in both wood and clay, and a creative-print artist who made his mark so firmly in the early days that today he is by acclamation president of the *Hanga* Association. His older brother, Hakutei Ishii (born 1882), is also a distinguished artist and a major figure in the beginnings of the creative print.

"Yamamoto was already in his fourth year when I entered the academy at Ueno," says Ishii, "but he lived at our house as one of the family, and few were ever as close to him as Hakutei and I. He was the first to combine great talent in both oil painting and wood engraving, and he was the first to make a creative print in Japan.

"There had been creative *hanga* before, not woodprints but etchings and lithographs. You can trace creative etchings back even before Meiji. The lithographic process came to Japan during early Meiji and a few men, my father among them, did some creative work with it. I don't mean that they were conscious of starting a

KANAE
YAMAMOTO

11

movement, but they did create a feeling, an atmosphere, and into this atmosphere came Kanae Yamamoto.

"Kanae made his first creative print in 1904. He had gone on a sketching trip to Choshi in Chiba and when he came back he made the print from a sketch of a fisherman in the costume they put on to celebrate a big catch. He carved with the technique of wood engraving but he used a Japanese-style block, cut with the grain. It wasn't a big print, maybe four by six inches. It was in two colors, and for his two blocks he carved both sides of the same board. I'm sure I have that block somewhere in the house. It would be interesting to run another print from it—but on second thought I don't think I'd want to. Wherever he is, Heaven or elsewhere, Kanae would probably raise violent objections." (The print is reproduced as print 3.)

"Hakutei published this print in the magazine *Myojo,* where he was an editor, labeling it a *toga,* a knife picture. It wasn't until several years later that they invented the word *hanga."*

Ishii's remark brings to mind one of Koshiro Onchi's stories which illustrates both the difficulties of the early days and the complexities of the language. The word *hanga* has the same pronunciation as an expression meaning "half picture." In 1915, after the word had been invented, a small group called the Tokyo *Hanga* Club held an exhibition. Every exhibition of that period had to be passed by a police board of censorship, and one of the prints appeared to the inspector to be unfinished. This suspicion was confirmed in his mind when he recalled that it had been called a *hanga,* which he interpreted to mean half picture. Holding that it was improper to exhibit unfinished work, he ordered the print down and, still unsatisfied, went to the artist's home and confiscated the block.

Yamamoto's early enthusiasm was contagious, and Hakutei Ishii found himself becoming nostalgic for the glories of *ukiyoe.* Remarking that "we cannot bear to stand by and see this death of an art which was once the pride of Japan," he published a series of prints called *Twelve Views of Tokyo.* In good *ukiyoe* tradition, these turned out to be pictures of beautiful women from different

12

sections of the city. Also in *ukiyoe* tradition, Hakutei, who lacked Yamamoto's training as a wood engraver, turned to artisans for help, but the day of the creative print had come, and Hakutei Ishii was one of the first to recognize it.

By the time Yamamoto graduated from Ueno, he was deeply excited about creative woodprints and was the driving force behind the whole movement. It was he who gave the early prints their distinctive look when he pioneered the use of the curved-blade chisel, which was the mark of creative *hanga* for many years. To *ukiyoe* artisans this chisel, with a blade shaped something like a flour scoop, was only a tool to clean up the block, but in Yamamoto's hands it became a major instrument of virtuosity, as demonstrated by *On the Deck* (print 1). There is a striking development from *Fisherman* (print 3) to *On the Deck*. *Fisherman* was carved as a wood engraver would carve, in the Western style, cutting out white lines against the black background. In *On the Deck* he pushed this concept much further, carving out the white to create not lines, but planes, shadows, and mass.

In 1907, Yamamoto, Hakutei Ishii, and a few others started the magazine *Hosun,* and for the four years of its life they filled its pages with their own creative *hanga* and comment. This slim magazine, whose title meant "a little thing," is the first great landmark of the creative-print movement, and with the group Pan, of which it was the unofficial voice, forms a fascinating chapter in the history of Japanese art in the early years of the century.

Pan achieved notoriety as a boisterous, uninhibited, saké-loving crowd of artists, but behind the rowdyism it was to the artists a serious effort to assimilate the new modernism of the West without sacrificing their Japanese nature. Devoted to *ukiyoe* and to the spirit which produced it, they chose a meeting place in what had been the heart of old Edo (the former name for Tokyo), close by the Sumida River, and here they came to grips with the issue which still plagues Japanese art. If they failed to gain a final solution to their problem, they at least recognized it, faced up to it, and more often than not gained temporary victory by drinking it under the table.

It probably goes without saying that they invited the attention of the police, who were only too inclined to see a socialist under every beret. The irreverence of their caricatures in *Hosun* (Yamamoto, who admired Hokusai, was not backward in this department) was a constant incitement to the official mind, but their greatest fame was achieved when, in the course of a party called to condole a couple of members on their imminent induction into the army, they draped the pictures of the new privates with black to signify their demise, a piece of blasphemy which was promptly splashed on the front pages by an offended newspaperman. The police and the military were furious, but the public thought it very funny.

In the years after his graduation, Yamamoto devoted himself almost entirely to creative *hanga,* and then in 1912, amid speculation that he was running away to heal a broken heart, he went to Paris. He stayed in Europe until late 1916 and artistically these years were among the most productive of his life. He sent back prints to repay those who had helped finance his journey and he supported himself by his prints and oils and his old skill at illustration by wood engraving. Many of his finest prints were made in Paris from 1912 to 1914, among them *On the Deck* (print 1), *A Small Bay in Brittany* (print 2), and *Yanchin,* a picture of three Chinese courtesans. He had another burst of activity just after he returned to Japan, including *Woman of Brittany* (print 5) and the Moscow prints (prints 6 and 7), the latter inspired by his homeward journey through Russia. That was a fateful journey for Yamamoto because he saw in Russia some schools for peasants which excited him about the possibilities of adult education for farmers. He lingered there, fascinated by those schools.

Back in Japan, he plunged again into the growing creative-print movement. He was the central figure in organizing the *hanga* artists into the association which still exists, and in preparing the association's first show, held during January 1919 at the Mitsukoshi Department Store in Tokyo's Nihonbasni. It was a good beginning, a big and successful exhibit of the work of twenty-five artists, including two Englishmen then resident in Japan, Bernard Leach and W. Westley Manning.

14

1. On the Deck (1912)   KANAE YAMAMOTO

And then in 1919 Yamamoto embarked on another crusade. He could not get over his dream of a school for farm people. He went to Shinshu, to the village of Oya where his father had practiced medicine. In that country, high in the central mountains, the long cold winters brought dullness and apathy, with little to do but sit in the *kotatsu,* the pit in the floor where the charcoal fire underneath the blankets kept at least the lower body warm. To Yamamoto this waste of life was an irresistible challenge. His solution was a school where the people could learn the kind of art and handicrafts which would both enrich their lives and make it possible for them to augment their meager incomes during the slack winter.

He gathered a staff of instructors and started an ambitious program of woodcarving, textile weaving and dyeing, and some painting and print-making. Yamamoto was not a man of small ideas, and he did not envision his school on a small scale. He solicited help from both government and private agencies, and among his largest grants were four thousand yen each from the Education Ministry, the Agriculture Ministry, and the Mitsubishi interests. These were annual pledges, and not inconsiderable money for those days when the yen was worth about half a dollar and the dollar rather more than it is today. But Yamamoto found it harder to maintain interest than to excite it in the first place. His big subsidies dwindled to half the original figure and, after five years, stopped. And in Oya the mayor of the village, who had been an enthusiastic supporter, went bankrupt. The school charged no fees, support was increasingly scarce, and finances became an overriding worry. Always there was the nagging necessity to hunt for patrons.

That was not his only trouble. Because he had gotten his idea in Russia, the police always suspected that he was teaching communism and continually harassed him on that score. Un'ichi Hiratsuka, who for a while taught frame-making at the school, recalls that when he was preparing for his first trip to Shinshu he received a letter from Yamamoto. Yamamoto described his difficulties with the police and diffidently asked Hiratsuka, who is deeply conservative but who likes to work in a Russian-style jacket, if he would forego that costume at Shinshu. And, he added, the police seemed to mistrust long hair and would Hiratsuka mind too much getting a haircut.

"Yamamoto was a fine artist but a terrible businessman," says Tsuruzo Ishii. "When he started the school I told him that he should restrict his activity to teaching art and crafts, but he thought he would fail if he couldn't prove to the farmers that they could make money out of what they were learning. So he was continually involved in trying to sell their products, and all these efforts lost money.

"It was the same with his other crusade. He threw himself into a campaign to change the methods of teaching art in the public schools. He called it free art, the idea being that students were to sketch from nature instead of copying the pictures in textbooks. Of course he stirred up a battle with the textbook people and old-line art teachers, but his campaign was finally scuttled by an unfortunate business deal: his only interest was to make a better quality of art supplies available to students, but the whole thing ended in bankruptcy. Both the Shinshu school and the free-art movement were good ideas doomed by bad management.

"I was always trying to get him to give up these crusades of his and do some painting. He was a stubborn and a dedicated man, but after fifteen years of struggling and with both ventures failing, he was tired out, and in 1935 he did settle down in Tokyo. For the first time since Paris he seriously worked at his own art. In the next five or six years he did some fine work, oils and water colors, and he climaxed this activity with a one-man show at Mitsukoshi in January 1940."

The show opened in an aura of good feeling. The antagonisms and bitterness of the past were forgotten, and both long-time friends and former enemies rallied around to celebrate his return to art with an impressive testimonial dinner. Yamamoto was in a happy and expansive mood when he rose to say: "I shall live until I'm eighty-five. I shall live until May of my eighty-fifth year. Therefore, I am going to sit back now, and drink saké, and paint to my heart's content."

He was a poor prophet. Two years later he was struck by a

cerebral hemorrhage, which ended his career. In the spring he was taken back to Shinshu in the hope that the mountains would aid his convalescence, but he never fully recovered, and he died in October 1946 at the age of sixty-four.

It was near the end of his illness that he got out of bed and took a hatchet to the blocks for his woodprints. He had carved them of solid *sakura* and undoubtedly many more prints could have been run off from them. If this was the thought that got him up to destroy them, it was in character. For a man who believed so deeply in creative prints it must have been anathema that somebody else might print from his blocks, and a final act of passionate conviction is a fitting end to his story.

That he was thwarted in this, as he had been so often before, is perhaps only consistent with the pattern of his life. Years before, when they were closing up the school at Oya, they had found there the blocks for his great print of Moscow (print 6). A friend who was helping asked for them, and Yamamoto gave them to him. Today there are plans to run some more prints from these blocks.

"What kind of man was he?"

Ishii reflected. "When an idea excited him he would bury himself in it. Sacrifice meant nothing. It was the same with creative *hanga,* his school, and his free-art movement. He was a selfless man, a passionate man, a man of great sensitivity. I guess if I had to describe him in one word it would be—artist."

2. *A Small Bay in Brittany (1913 ?)*

KANAE
YAMAMOTO

3. *Fisherman (1904)*

4. *French Pastoral in Spring* (1913 ?)

KANAE
YAMAMOTO

5. *Woman of Brittany* (1920)

KANAE
YAMAMOTO

6. *Moscow Street* (1916 ?)

7. *Moscow* (1917 ?)

3
KOSHIRO
ONCHI

AFTER YAMAMOTO TURNED TO OTHER ENTHU-siasms leadership fell to such men as Koshiro Onchi (1891–1955). With a scant ten years between Yamamoto's birth and his, he represented a new generation of men to whom *hanga* was a career and not a bypath (sometimes passionately pursued, but still a bypath). Onchi's span of activity reached back to the days of the magazine *Hosun,* and in all that time there was never any question but that he was a *hanga* artist.

He made up his mind to that almost as soon as he made up his mind to be an artist, both decisions being part of a pattern of revolt that carried him as far as possible from the kind of life he was brought up to.

His father, happily on the other side of the fence from Yamamoto's grandfather, was a ruggedly conservative member of Emperor Meiji's highly formal court. A gentleman of the old school, uncompromisingly honest and unswervingly loyal, he was a favorite with the emperor. He served for a time as the court's master of ceremonies and then at the emperor's request he took over the education and discipline of the three young princes who were destined to wed the emperor's daughters. Koshiro, youngest of Onchi's four sons, was raised with the princes in the rigid atmosphere that characterized old-line education of members of the imperial family. Late in life he recalled one treasonous moment when he disrupted that atmosphere by slapping the young Prince Higashikuni, though he couldn't remember what the prince did to deserve it. One of the last jobs of book design which Onchi completed before his death was the autobiography of the prince, now plain mister since he lost his title after the war.

Notwithstanding the slap, Onchi shared the princes' education under his stern and domineering father. He studied the Chinese classics with emphasis on Confucian doctrine, he spent long hours over his calligraphy, and he learned the classic theatre art of the nobility, Noh. He never forgot such roles as Yoshitsune in *Funa-Benkei* but he regarded Noh as fugitive from a museum, and the last time he saw a play was when, out of filial duty, he attended the farewell performance of a man to whom his father had been patron.

It was planned that young Onchi would be a doctor, and he entered a German middle school in Tokyo which specialized in premedical training. While he was there one elder brother died of a heart attack and another of tuberculosis, and when a sister died in the same span of two years, Onchi lost whatever faith and interest he had once had in medicine. His early interest in art had been sternly suppressed by his father, but after the shock of losing three of his children the old man relented, and at the age of seventeen Onchi entered the government art academy at Ueno.

However, any assumption that he was now happy in his chosen field would be premature. He was by this time in full revolt against his strict upbringing, and the authorities at Ueno bore the brunt of it. He shunned their compulsory athletics, he attended classes only when felt like it, and he painted as he chose. If this meant doing nudes in grey and blue instead of the warm fleshy tones demanded by the academy instructors, that was the way it was, and Onchi was not at all impressed by arguments that at least while he was a student he must paint as his instructors directed. On top of all this he was neglecting his oils for the absurd heresy of creative prints. In this atmosphere of mutual antagonism it is remarkable that Onchi's career at Ueno lasted as long as three years. When he was invited to leave, his departure was a double farewell, for at the same time he abandoned oil painting. From then on he devoted himself to *hanga*.

His decision to make *hanga* his career was influenced partly by the work of Yamamoto and the others in *Hosun,* but even more by the work of Europeans like Wassily Kandinsky and Edvard Munch, whose prints were then being reproduced in Tokyo. "I was especially impressed by Munch's expression of human feeling," Onchi said, "not his form but his content."

During the next ten or fifteen years creative prints and Onchi grew up together. He threw himself into the movement, and his fighting spirit gloried in the fact that the whole art world was lined up in opposition.

"At first we were simply ignored," he said, "and then, when we couldn't be ignored, we were ridiculed. All the shows were run by oil painters. If we were allowed to submit our work, it was hung on some remote wall and judged in the same category as the oils, by a jury composed of oil painters. Of course we got nowhere. The critics? They acted as if we didn't exist."

To further the cause he poured his energy and whatever money he could find into a series of art and literary magazines, most of which expired after a few issues. But he kept on fighting, and since he loved a good fight he had a fine time.

He didn't seriously try to earn money to support his family until the devastating earthquake of 1923 jolted him into a new sense of responsibility. His wife still recalls her excitement when he received fifty yen for a book design, the pleasant shock when she realized

23

that her husband, too, could make money. Though he started late, from then on he earned a very comfortable living as one of Japan's foremost book designers. His early training in calligraphy may have contributed something too, for Onchi was regarded as a superlative designer of lettering, if that word may be stretched to include the complex ideographs used both in China and Japan.

Much as he revolted against it, his early environment must have been decisive in yet another respect, for his tastes were essentially aristocratic. He shunned Yamamoto's school for farmers and did not hesitate to express his displeasure with peasant art, an attitude that did not endear him to the powerful *mingei* group, which has sponsored the great revival of folk arts and crafts.

Onchi was deeply Japanese, but from the beginning of his career any overt Japanese influence on his work was negligible. He liked that considerable portion of Japanese art which is dominated by simplicity and elegance, but he never turned back to it for stimulation, and against *ukiyoe* he conducted full-scale rebellion. Elise Grilli, art critic of the *Nippon Times,* put it this way: "Onchi delighted in flaunting the conventions of *ukiyoe* prints. The meticulous craftsmanship, the virtuosity of line, the hair-raisingly painstaking printing from twenty or thirty separate blocks, the finicky precision in overlapping the colors, and, in recent times, the overwhelming cleverness in naturalistic representation—all this he threw out the window with a single toss and a hearty laugh. Now he could breathe again, freed from the claptrap of academic accretions."

Though he never went to Europe—his only trips outside Japan were to Formosa and later, in 1939, as an army artist to China—he was consistently oriented to the European rather than the Japanese, to the new rather than the old. This orientation is obviously reflected in his abstract work. In deference to realists like Yamamoto he made realistic prints for exhibition until World War II loosened his inhibitions, but abstract art had always been his paramount interest, and during the last ten or fifteen years of his life his output was almost entirely abstract. It was in these later years that he wrote: "Abstract art is now, as it should be, the main way of art, and I hope that our civilization soon comes to realize this. My

24

work falls short of my expectations, short of what I want it to be, but I keep it up as one pioneer doing his part to cultivate this vast land. If my work happens to be poor, the fault is mine alone and not that of the method."

To Onchi *hanga* was not only a great medium but one uniquely suited to abstract art. He stressed this in his book, *The Modern Hanga of Japan:*

"Among the mediums of *hanga* the one most removed from the brush painting is the woodcut. A woodcut is best when the chisel in the wood is used most naturally. The virtue of *hanga* lies in the certainty that it comes from a creative process which permits no sham. Unlike brush painting, it allows no wavering of the hand. It is honest—sham and errors show. Some liberty may be allowed in the registry but so little that it, like the carving, is a process which permits no delusion ... *hanga* rejects the accidental and rejects ornamentation ... and it contains the most constructive process in graphic art, the advantage of superimposing pictures. For this reason *hanga* is probably the most suitable method yet found for the expression of modern art, which lays stress on construction."

His emphasis on abstract art gave rise to one misunderstanding, a common belief that he did not regard the ability to draw as important to the *hanga* artist. Onchi could draw with mastery. "Of course," he said, "one must be able to draw and sketch to make realistic prints. For abstracts, on the other hand, the important thing is composition and construction."

It was chiefly in his abstract prints that Onchi pioneered new techniques and probed the use of new materials. A print must be made with a block, to be sure, but this definition does not prescribe how the block is to be made. For his printing blocks Onchi used paper, cardboard, string, a rubber heel, charcoal, textiles, the fins of a fish, leaves—anything that came to hand and caught his lively imagination. He sometimes laughed at his own improvisations and accused himself of cheating, but this free use of materials remains one of his greatest contributions.

Michener has lighted up the whole creative-print movement with his story of how Onchi made one of the greatest of the modern

25

prints, the brilliant portrait of his friend the poet Sakutaro Hagiwara (print 10). However, a look at how he made the lovely *Poem Number 22: Leaf and Clouds* (print 14) shows him at work on a more typical (because non-realistic) print and illustrates his innovations in technique and materials.

Onchi started with a pencil sketch of his basic design. The sketch, same size as the finished print, was a composition based on four different forms and a natural leaf. Having finished his design, he cut the four forms from waxed paper which he had carefully saved from the wrapping around cigarette cartons (Onchi was an inveterate saver, couldn't bear to throw anything away). The accompanying diagram shows these forms in proportionate size and numbered in the order in which he printed with them.

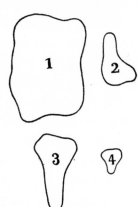

His fifth "block" was a natural leaf from a *yuzuriha* tree. These glossy leaves are often used with oranges and white paper to decorate doorways at New Year's time, and when this attractively worm-eaten specimen had appeared some prior New Year, Onchi had spotted it and added it to his hoard. In order to print from it he glued it to a thin board only a little larger than the leaf.

When he was ready to print, Onchi placed his sketch underneath a piece of clear glass so that the design showed through to give him a "map." Taking waxed-paper form number 1, he brushed ink on it, putting most of the ink close to the edge of the paper. For his ink he used regular *sumi,* adding a little vegetable mucilage called *nori.* He placed the paper form on the glass, matching its position with the design beneath and with the inked side down against the glass. Then he took the paper which he wanted to print and laid it on the glass over the waxed-paper form. Since he had no *kento,* to position his paper he matched the corners with those of the sketch beneath. Finally he took his *baren* and rubbed the back of his paper just as though he were printing from a wood

26

8. *Objet Number 2 (1954)*   KOSHIRO ONCHI

block. The ink, pressed between the glass and the impermeable waxed-paper form, oozed out around the edges of the form, and as it did so it printed on the paper above. Because Onchi printed on a fairly hard-surfaced, non-absorbent paper called *kyokushi,* the pattern of the irregular ooze was in some places quite wide.

That much done, Onchi removed the waxed-paper form, wiped the glass clean, applied some more ink to the same form, placed it about an inch lower than he had the first time, and repeated the process.

Then he used form number 2 in the same manner, printing with it in three different positions. Form number 3 he used once, and with it he introduced his only color other than black, a golden tan in a water-color paint. Form number 4, the small triangle, was printed three times with ink much blacker than that used on the bigger forms.

Last of all came the leaf, mounted on its small board. Onchi removed the glass because the board might skid on it, and positioned this block directly on the design, leaf up. Jet-black ink was brushed on the leaf, and then he placed his paper down on top of it as though it were a wood block, again matching corners with the sketch in lieu of a *kento* and printing with his *baren* in normal fashion.

If the finished print passed his critical inspection, Onchi stamped his name (here spelled Onzi—he made no virtue of consistency in spelling his own name in Roman letters) in the lower right corner (it can be seen in the reproduction just under the stem), and the work was complete. It is safe to say that it had been work undertaken in joy, carried through with exuberance, and finished swiftly. He tried to finish a job before the fun went out of it. "I have a good life," he liked to say, "and I want that to show in my work."

Over a period of a year and a half Onchi made ten copies of this print, and then, although he saved the handsome leaf, he destroyed his paper blocks. This was a large edition for him, because when he had made one print that satisfied him the act of creation was complete, and much as it might exasperate those who tried to collect his prints, he usually felt an overpowering urge to drop the matter there.

27

In speaking of the portrait of Sakutaro Hagiwara, Michener has told of the pains that Onchi took to find the right paper. He printed that portrait on four different papers with results ranging from superb to worthless, and it was the paper that told the story. Said Onchi: "I give half the credit for the world-wide fame of *ukiyoe* color prints to the wonderful *hosho* and *masagami* papers on which they were made. For example, it's the paper which is responsible for the sensuous beauty of the women's complexions."

For most of his prints Onchi preferred a finely textured, firm but absorbent, white paper called *edogawa,* but true *edogawa* hasn't been made since the war, and like many of the other artists he mostly used *torinoko.*

Present-day *torinoko* has been criticized as being a short-lived paper and therefore unsuitable for making prints, but it is popular among the artists nevertheless. In the old days vellum-like *torinoko* made from the short silky fiber of the *gampi* plant was one of Japan's most magnificent papers. Unfortunately, *gampi* grows only wild in the mountains and cannot be cultivated, so that the supply is scarce and the paper made from it is expensive. Moreover, *gampi* paper is basically unsuited for making prints because it is not absorbent. The paper called *torinoko* today is an imitation, made from various combinations of *mitsumata* and pulp. It comes in a number of grades depending on the amount of pulp which has been added, and of course, the more pulp the cheaper the paper. Grades 1 and 2 are usually considered too pure, that is they do not contain enough pulp to give the paper the proper absorbency. Grade 3 is the most popular and grade 4 is also used. Since *torinoko* is the paper used to face Japanese doors *(fusuma),* it comes in rolls about six feet by three, so that there is very little limitation on the size of a print. It can also be obtained in sheets. Some of the artists, like Jun'ichiro Sekino, order a specially made *torinoko,* of a quality particularly adapted to prints.

Because of Onchi's great range, it is not easy to select a few out-standing prints, but among his portraits one must name *Sakutaro Hagiwara* (print 10), *Shizuya Fujikake,* and *Impression of a Violinist* (frontispiece); in his realistic vein, *Among the Rocks* (print 9), *The Temple of Confucius in Formosa,* and *Ripples,* a study of a Chinese washerwoman; and from his abstract work, *Objet Number 2* (print 8), *Lyric Number 13: Melancholy of Japan* (print 12), *Poem Number 8–1: Butterfly* (print 13), and *Poem Number 22: Leaf and Clouds* (print 14).

It was no mere whim that caused Onchi to name some of his prints "Poems," for, like his friend Hagiwara, Onchi was a poet. Almost every one of his major prints was coupled with a poem, free in form, subtle and allusive, often as abstract as the print it attended.

Artist and poet, his emotions were close to the surface, and they quickly welled up in bursts of feeling. In his notes he set down how he came to make the tragic mask called *Impression of a Violinist* (frontispiece). It was 1947 and he had been invited by his good friend William Hartnett to one of the concerts that Hartnett arranged for Occupation audiences. The evening was a triumph for Hartnett because he had been able to persuade Nejiko Suwa, one of Japan's great violinists, to play. Miss Suwa, a proud person and a perfectionist who seldom plays in public because of the impossibly high standards she sets for herself, had suffered in the war, and Onchi felt the undertones as he watched her play to an American audience at a time when Japan's defeat was still fresh. "A harsh electric light showed the strain in her face," he wrote, "and I saw tragedy there. Suddenly my eyes were blurred with tears."

Though Onchi was easily moved, he usually overflowed with the joy of life. He loved to sing, to others if they'd listen, to himself if they wouldn't. He sang even in his last illness, but his repertoire gradually narrowed to *Jesus Loves Me,* in either Japanese or English, and one song of yearning for the homeland which was sung so much during the war that the words stuck with him. "I try to sing other songs," he would explain, "but they always come out as one of those two."

Onchi's death was a blow to his fellow artists. They miss the healthy ferment of his work, which kept them all on their toes, and they miss the man—his surging creative force, his bigness of

KOSHIRO ONCHI

spirit, his imagination, wit, and integrity. Still he left them a creed of vitality, of honesty, and of freedom, and it seems safe to say that, as long as they look to it, the movement will neither stagnate nor crystallize. That, of course, is good. That is a legacy worth leaving.

9. *Among the Rocks* (1929)

KOSHIRO
ONCHI

10. *Portrait of Sakutaro
Hagiwara (1943)*

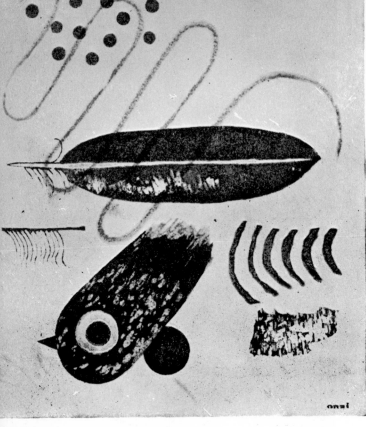

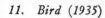
11. *Bird (1935)*

12. *Lyric Number 13:*
    Melancholy of
    Japan (1952)

KOSHIRO
ONCHI

KOSHIRO
ONCHI

13. Poem Number 8-1:
Butterfly (1948)

14. Poem Number 22:
Leaf and Clouds (1953)

4
UN'ICHI
HIRATSUKA

UN'ICHI HIRATSUKA (BORN 1895) IS QUIET where Onchi was exuberant, serious where Onchi was witty, precise where Onchi was daring. Onchi rejected classical Japanese art, Hiratsuka plumbs it. Onchi had within him the flame of a revolutionary, Hiratsuka is deeply traditional. It was inevitable that these two very different men should have been sometimes impatient with each other, but when they pooled their complementary talents in the common cause of creative *hanga* they made a formidable team.

Hiratsuka is a small, compact man. A high forehead, with grey hair brushed straight back, sets off a sharply molded, ascetic face with its accents of a cropped mustache and a little tuft under his lower lip. He, his wife, and their attractive artist daughter live in

35

their studio home in Tokyo's Mejiro district; another daughter is living in Washington, D. C., happily married to an American who met her when he came to Tokyo by courtesy of the U.S. Navy.

Here is Hiratsuka's story as he tells it: "I come from Matsue, the old town near the Japan Sea where Lafcadio Hearn lived and taught school. My grandfather was an architect of houses and temples and there were always carpenters around our place, so I grew up with a feeling for wood and tools. The first carving I became aware of was the work of the seal-makers, the men who make the big and little hand-stamps without which nothing in Japan can be authenticated. I started by carving Chinese characters, as they did, but I soon went on to pictures. That was the period when those avant-garde art magazines *Myojo* and *Shirakaba* were introducing the postimpressionists to Japan. I studied these magazines avidly, so my early influences were all Western.

"I hadn't really made up my mind to be an artist till, when I was eighteen, Hakutei Ishii came to Matsue. I studied with him for the month he taught there, and when he praised one of my water colors, that did it. I waited until I was twenty-one and then I came to Tokyo and enrolled in the art school of Saburosuke Okada. Okada was a great academician and I stayed in his school for five or six years, but I felt much closer to Ishii, and it was to him that I kept going to show my work and get advice. He was really my teacher. I've never stopped learning from him.

"Those were the days when the creative-print movement was being born. Kanae Yamamoto and Ishii were the heart of it, and when one day I told Ishii that I had always been interested in making prints, I hit on something he was deeply excited about. He insisted that the day of the creative print was not far off and urged me to study print-making seriously. On his advice I went to the artisan Bonkotsu Igami to study the technique of carving."

Hiratsuka agrees that it was a little strange to find a traditional *ukiyoe* artisan associating with the Western-style artists who were leading the movement toward creative prints. "Igami was very different from most of the artisans," he says. "He was a bohemian soul who liked artists, and he got along fine with the

36

creative group. He and Ishii and Kanae Yamamoto were in the center of the group called Pan. They specialized in saké parties and such diversions, and once they put on a play in which Igami, who stuttered terrifically, brought down the house because he never could get started on his first line. Anyway, Igami set me to learning how to carve the blocks for reproductions of traditional *ukiyoe* color prints. He made me work hard on difficult carving techniques like the hair on the face, and he forbade me to work on my own pictures. I had six months of this training, and then he told me I had the fundamentals and dismissed me to go my own way."

Hiratsuka first studied Japanese art after coming to Tokyo. "Ishii convinced me that an artist was well advised not to depend on making a living from the sale of his pictures, and so for some time I helped edit various art magazines. In this work I had to learn something about Japanese art and what I learned became a tremendous influence. I could never be the same once under the sway of the prints of Moronobu, or the Buddhist prints and paintings of the Heian era (794–1185), or the paintings of Taiga, Buson, and, most of all, Sesshu."

All of this work is in black and white, as is Hiratsuka's best. He says: "To me black and white have always been the most beautiful of the colors. For some subjects I feel that I must go into other colors, but I know that generally my work weakens when I do.

"With its special beauties, a black and white has special problems. To borrow musical terms, a black and white must have a rhythm of line and mass and a harmony of straight lines and curves. One of the great difficulties is to make the white space live. I know that's a problem for every artist everywhere, but it's particularly acute for a Japanese artist because his white space remains untreated, the natural surface of his paper. The handling of white space is different in every one of my pictures."

Hiratsuka's distinctive line is not smooth and flowing. It has a jagged edge which seems to freeze movement, to stop time, and to give the moment a sense of solid permanence. He gets this effect, which he first used in 1936 in a print of Matsue castle, by poking sideways along the line with a square-end chisel. He says:

37

"This rough line came out of my search for greater strength and a feeling of solid mass. It's for the same reason that I make my black as intense as I can get it: my black ink is the very finest *sumi* from Kyoto, and I make impression after impression until the color seeps deep into the paper.

"I have always tried for power and strength in my pictures. I have done some Japanese-style brush painting, but I always come back to prints because I feel that they are stronger. I'm convinced that, had advanced block printing existed in Sesshu's day, he would have deserted brush painting."

Hiratsuka has a special feeling for the earliest prints made in Japan, the Buddhist prints of the Heian era. He believes that they were carved by the sculptors who were making the religious statues, and thinks that this accounts for their freshness and naïveté. For years he has been preparing a history of these prints. This has led him to a study of ancient tiles, for he explains that since these tiles were pressed (one might say, printed) from carved wood forms, they bear a close relationship to prints. The first tile-makers came to Japan from Korea in 588, and prints were introduced from China a couple of hundred years later. Both came on the wave of Buddhist culture, the tiles as an essential to the building of proper temples and the prints as an aid to worship.

Hiratsuka has assembled a collection of more than five thousand tiles and fragments, Japanese, Chinese, and Korean, and in addition, he has hundreds of rubbings made at sites in China and Korea, these being expedient when he found tiles too big or too permanently attached to carry home. In such rubbings he finds the strength and solidity he wants to express in his prints. He points out that these rubbings reveal not a smooth but a rough line, like that he is using. He thinks that the Frenchman Georges Braque has felt the same influence. Braque once requested some Korean paper and used it to make an etching, later exhibited in Tokyo, which reminded Hiratsuka of the rubbings from Chinese tiles.

Hiratsuka sums up the effect of Western and Japanese influences on his own work in this way: "Western art gave me my technique but Japanese art gave me my approach. So my light isn't real

38

15. *At the Foot of Mt. Amagi (1954)*   UN'ICHI HIRATSUKA

sunlight, and my shadows aren't real shadows. They are creations of my own and I use them freely to help me get at the soul of whatever subject I'm handling." He agrees that his earlier work was somewhat more Western than his later. "It's like peeling an onion," he says. "You slough off the outer layers of technical convention to get at the heart of the matter. Today's realism is based on an impression of nature, or perhaps it's better to say an inspiration from nature. And I think that the abstract artist should draw his inspiration from nature too. That's why I like the work of Onchi and some of the others in printing from actual objects like leaves.

"I have done some experimenting of my own," he goes on, "chiefly to find new uses for the carving tools. In an early period I used only V-shaped knives, which make thin lines like a wood engraving. Now I cut almost exclusively with flat blades, some square-end, some angled."

He always cuts his blocks from solid wood, not veneer. Mostly he uses *katsura*, but for small prints he may use *sakura*, and occasionally he cuts a block from *ho*, which is about halfway between *sakura* and *katsura* in hardness.

He prefers to print on *hodomura*, a fine *kozo* paper made at Echizen in Fukui Prefecture. This paper contains no mucilage binder and he never moistens it in printing. He does moisten *torinoko* paper when he uses it.

Since a black and white print uses a single color it is made from a single block. Hiratsuka does not cut a *kento* on such a block, and once the paper is placed on the block it is kept there until the print is finished, one portion being held in place while he works on another part. However, when he makes color prints, which require several blocks, he puts a *kento* on his blocks and prints in the same manner as a traditional *ukiyoe* artisan.

Once in a while, when he accepts a commission to do a calendar or some similar project which requires a large number of prints, he turns the printing over to an artisan. In his younger days Hiratsuka himself occasionally assumed the role of artisan if an artist of kindred spirit wanted to try his hand at designing prints. One such artist was Bernard Leach, and Hiratsuka also carved the blocks and did the printing for some of the prints in a quite distinguished series designed by the prominent oil painter Sotaro Yasui, who thereafter strongly advocated print-making as valuable training in line and color.

Hiratsuka tries to make one point clear. He says: "I am not a wood-print artist, I am an artist." He finds the same basic problems of drawing and deformation in any attempt to create a picture, whether by print or by oil, and he says he can't understand why more Japanese oil painters don't follow the European example and also make *hanga*—prints, etchings, lithographs.

"An artist should be versatile as to media," he says. Japanese artists who go to France learn this, and usually come back with *hanga* better than their oils."

Hiratsuka attributes this current single-minded emphasis on oil very largely to the influence of the government-sponsored art show. The official attitude is apparently one of overawed respect for oil, and, of all countries in the world, Japan's government-sponsored art show has no *hanga* section, prints being relegated to a wall or two mixed in with the oils. The situation is worsened by the fact that there is no *hanga* course in the government art academy at Ueno in Tokyo.

Hiratsuka has long been a leader in the fight to change this state of affairs. For a while, before and during the war, classes in prints and etchings were established at Ueno—Hiratsuka taught the print class—but one of those storms which periodically strike the art world caused both to be discontinued in 1944. After another ten years of fighting, the Education Ministry has finally agreed to re-establish a *hanga* course in the academy, and there is hope that it will get under way in 1956.

The battle for fair representation in the government art show still goes on, and in the meantime most of the print artists exhibit elsewhere and have pledged not to submit any work to the government show, though this is by no means a solid front. On the other hand, many of the artists have joined one of the few art associations which have proven hospitable to *hanga,* the Kokuga-kai. This group was founded by a number of progressive Japanese-style painters led

40

by Bakusen Tsuchida, and their prospectus invited print artists to join with them. Though the association was later taken over by oil painters, among them Ryuzaburo Umehara, its character did not change, for Umehara, a pupil of Renoir, shared the same progressive views in art as Tsuchida. It was Tsuchida, in 1924, who asked Hiratsuka to take the lead in encouraging *hanga* artists to join, and it was Umehara, in 1931, who promoted the establishment of a separate *hanga* section, the first and until recently the only such section in a Japanese art association. "For the first time," says Hiratsuka, "*hanga* artists had a whole room instead of a wall, and *hanga* artists did the judging instead of oil painters; it was a big step forward. In 1936 I invited Onchi to join and he gave the group a wider range. The association has always tried to have both the traditional and the modern point of view represented in each section." Most of the artists discussed in this book are, or have been, members of Kokuga-kai.

Hiratsuka is one of the first modern woodblock artists to make a living from the sale of his prints, and this, along with his steady production, makes him the "old pro" of the group. He thinks that by now he must have made about two thousand pictures, and he still has the blocks for most of them. Selecting prints from this great output is a matter of personal taste, but in addition to those reproduced here one must include *The Bunraku Doll Yaoya O-Shichi* (the print Michener chose for *The Floating World*), *Stone Buddha of Usuki,* and *Ikaruga Temple in the Early Autumn*. All these are in black and white; among his loveliest color prints is one which catches the distinctive beauty of his homeland, *The Pine Grove of Tsuda at Matsue.*

His editions usually run about fifty for landscapes and thirty for other subjects, but in at least one case it has gone much higher: the rugged portrait of the militant Buddhist priest Nichiren (print 16). "Making that print is a sort of religious act for me," he says, smiling. "I have set myself to do ten thousand copies." So far the count is about a thousand. "That leaves quite a number to do—but I don't worry about it," he adds with a twinkle. "What I don't get done here I shall do in Heaven."

UN'ICHI
HIRATSUKA

16. *Nichiren
Shonin (1931)*

17. *Rakan Temple in
the Rain (1935)*

18. *Sutra Repository of Iwaya-dera (1940)*

UN'ICHI
HIRATSUKA

19. *Stone Buddhist Image (1946)*

20.   *Nandaimon (1937)*

UN'ICHI HIRATSUKA

21.   *The Innermost Temple of Koyasan (1941)*

5
SEMPAN MAEKAWA

SEMPAN MAEKAWA (BORN 1888) RECALLS AN additional element in the early movement toward creative prints. "Those of us who were making prints in those first days," he remembers, "were doing it partly in a spirit of resistance, an urge to do something the Japanese way in the face of the new passion for oil painting." Maekawa has been doing it the Japanese way ever since. "Of the men of his generation," says Robert T. Paine, Jr., of the Boston Museum of Fine Arts, "he has best preserved a Japanese nature, a broad humaneness of subject matter"—and with it a style that, apart from a noticeable trend toward simplification, has changed very little since he made his first print. "My style is part of me," Maekawa says. "I couldn't change even if I wanted to." He looks

45

on with approval as other artists experiment, but he leaves experimentation to them.

Maekawa was born to a family of Kyoto shopkeepers, but on his mother's side there was a long line of artisans in the crafts which have always thrived in the old capital—lacquerware, metalwork, and textile-dyeing. "My mother liked to draw," says Maekawa, "and I think I picked it up from her. When I was about seventeen or eighteen I made up my mind to be an artist. I went for a while to a private art school, and then when I was twenty-four I came to Tokyo." He landed a job on a magazine of cartoons called, in no doubt sincere flattery, *Puck*. *Puck* was a contemporary of *Hosun*, and, like it, gave work to many young artists, some of whom, like Kanae Yamamoto and Tsuruzo Ishii, appeared in both.

Maekawa hit Tokyo in 1911. Shortly thereafter Kunzo Minami, the oil painter, returned after several years of study in Paris, enormously impressed by the European excitement over Japan's traditional *ukiyoe* and enthusiastic about making prints himself as continental artists were doing. Back in Japan, Minami became another of the leaders of the new creative-print movement and was probably the first artist to hold an exhibition of his prints. Excited by Minami's work, Maekawa started to experiment, but he didn't actually publish a print until he was invited to participate in the 1919 show.

Like almost all of the early artists, he was self-taught. The worlds of traditional print-making and of the new creative movement were far apart, and very few men bridged them as Hiratsuka did, acting on the sound advice of Hakutei Ishii. Of course everybody knew the basic processes, and probably many had spent hours watching the artisans at work, as Maekawa had when he was a boy. But the spirit of the new movement, the militant creed that an artist should make his own prints, did not encourage learning from the craftsmen of the old school. Maekawa used the books that were beginning to appear, but mostly it was a process of time-consuming trial and error. "It took me ten years to learn technique," he says. "Later I got acquainted with some artisans and found they could have taught me the same things in a few hours."

During a good share of his career he was primarily an illustrator,

22. *Kyoto Flower Vendor (1951)*   SEMPAN MAEKAWA

and made only three or four prints a year for exhibition. "I made only three or four copies of those," he says, "and seldom sold one—usually ended up giving them away. I remember that the first year the government show accepted prints—that was 1927—I entered a print and it surprised me by selling. But creative prints were small and amateurish in those days. I was always preaching that we had to make them bigger and better.

"We've come a long way since then, but I had faith that we would. When Jun'ichiro Sekino arrived from the country twenty years ago he came to talk with me about his plans, and I encouraged him. 'Ten years from now,' I told him, 'you'll be able to make a living from your prints.' Ten years later he came back to report. 'I cannot,' he said, 'make a living.' I don't think I've ever apologized as much as I did on that occasion. It was only a little later that things began to look up for him, but it wasn't until the Americans came that creative prints really caught on. The Japanese still don't understand—they persecute *hanga*."

About midway in his career Maekawa was able to shift his emphasis and devote the greater effort to making prints, but he still does some illustration and cover design. ("Things are different from what they once were," he notes with satisfaction. "Now the publishers come to me.") His work as an illustrator has probably been a strong influence on his art, preserving his warm human approach in both style and subject matter. On the other hand, it is easy to confuse cause and effect in these matters and it may be Maekawa's innate humaneness that has made him a successful illustrator.

People are his main interest, the ordinary people of Japan, and although he sometimes shows them at work, he likes best to catch them when they are enjoying themselves. High in any list of Japanese pleasures are hot-spring baths and the traditional festivals of the country, so it is no accident that these are prominent in his work. Among his best prints are *A Spa* (print 26), *An Inn at Kamisuwa* (print 24), *Autumn in a Mountain Village, Cherry-Viewing Dance*—the same subject was later redone for a subscription series as *Cherry Festival* (print 25)—*Plum Orchard* (print 27), *Shadow-Picture Play,* and the recent, gay *Bon Odori.* He is also in top form with figures, beginning with a series of workingwomen done before the war and continuing with a progressively bolder approach through *Kyoto Flower Vendor* (print 22) to *Bird in Hand* (print 28).

Some of his pleasantest prints are found only in a series of handsome books, three published and two projected, devoted to his connoisseur's selection from the country's hundreds of hot-spring resorts. There is also a series of small books on a variety of topics ranging from landscapes to children's games. Both series were started during the war, when Maekawa evacuated with a publisher friend to Okayama, in the southwestern part of the main island of Honshu. The publisher brought along a supply of fine paper and Maekawa put it to good use.

When not out scouting hot springs, Maekawa lives with his wife in a quiet residential district in Tokyo. A man so modest he was unable to produce a photograph of himself, he is nevertheless a photographer's dream subject: the well-lined face of a man who loves the outdoors, lively eyes darting through glasses halfway down his nose and usually amused at what they see, angled eyebrows accentuating the quizzical look.

He is a refreshing personality because he seems to be doing, without trumpeting, exactly what he wants to do. His work has a fresh, naïve style, liberally salted with a sense of humor, and completely identified with the wood. Maekawa carries no torch for other media and, except for a brief fling with linoleum cuts, has never strayed from woodprints. "Etching? wood engraving? painting?—they're simply not agreeable to me," he says. "To me the wood-print quality is everything. Even calligraphy made with a brush is never wholly satisfying: I like a character only when it has been cut in wood."

In his early prints Maekawa, like the others, used only curved chisels (they were almost the badge of the early creative-print artist), but he is credited with being the first to break away. Now he carves exclusively with flat chisels, angled or square-edged. Mostly he makes his blocks of plywood faced with *shina*, although for some prints he uses solid blocks of *katsura*. His style is basically simple, and as a rule he cuts away the whole top layer of wood with very little attempt at shading, so that his blocks are clean, neat, and a joy to see.

He starts with a fairly free drawing, which he doesn't allow to restrict him as he carves. He pastes the drawing on the wood and cuts the block for the basic color. He makes an impression of this block and pastes it on wood as a guide in cutting the block for another color. In this way he is sure that his blocks will match up, and he proceeds in the same manner until he has finished all his blocks.

He prints on *torinoko* paper number 3 or 4, sizing his own paper with animal glue. Maekawa rarely moistens his paper before he prints, explaining that he likes to get his color with one stroke of the *baren* and consequently applies such heavy pressure that the paper might tear if it were moistened. Also unlike most artists, he rarely uses paste on his blocks or in his colors. He uses both water colors and poster colors.

His editions commonly run to about ten copies, sometimes going higher. "But generally," says Maekawa, "I tire of a print after I've made ten of it." And it is easy to picture him at this point, putting away his blocks and colors and taking off into the country, where a hot spring beckons.

23. *Factory District* (1929)

SEMPAN MAEKAWA

24. *An Inn at Kamisuwa* (1932)

25. *Cherry Festival (1941)*

SEMPAN MAEKAWA

26. *A Spa (1949)*

27. *Plum Orchard (1943)*

SEMPAN MAEKAWA

28. *Bird in Hand (1955)*

6
KIYOSHI
SAITO

OF THE MEN OF THE NEXT GENERATION, Kiyoshi Saito (born 1907) is probably best known. He produces more prints than any of the other artists and his editions usually sell out. His print sales, coupled with the demand for his magazine illustrations and commercial-art designs, have made possible a new house on the outskirts of Tokyo, where he works and lives with his wife and their teen-age daughter. His success somehow seems consistent with the man, for short, dark-skinned Saito has the quietly purposeful air of a thorough professional.

He describes himself as a frustrated oil painter, a remark which signifies that the creative-print movement has come of age. Certainly that is the full turn of the wheel from the early artists who wanted

53

to make prints but couldn't afford to neglect their oils for such an unprofitable sideline. Says Saito: "I haven't worked at it for more than three years but I still feel that I'm fundamentally an oil painter. For me, the joy of making a print is not in working with the materials but in creating the design. After all, with each stroke of the brush I improve as an artist, but with each cut of the chisel I improve only as an artisan."

Having raised the subject of artisans, Saito explains his position: "It's not that I object to artisans in principle. I'm perfectly willing that they copy my simpler things. But when I'm trying for a new or complicated effect I have to do the work myself even though I don't especially enjoy it." And he goes on: "I'm amused—and a little annoyed—by people who talk about some of my effects as though they were happy accidents. These people seem to think we modern artists let our medium control us. I scheme and work and sweat over my prints. Making a woodcut is much too strenuous to let accidents determine results."

Saito is not subject to easy classification and perhaps Onchi's broad category of "modern realist" is as descriptive as any. He rejects academic art in no uncertain terms and, on the other hand, although he often likes abstract art as done by others, he says that he has no desire to do abstracts, that for him forms must originate in nature.

He names Redon, Munch, and Gauguin as his strongest influences. "From the moment I first saw their work," he says, "I've been attracted by their romanticism, their exoticism, and their mysticism. I feel that my own work interprets this same mysticism in today's idiom." Closer to home, there is no doubt but that Onchi was a potent factor in Saito's development.

Speaking of *ukiyoe*, Saito describes his first reaction to Harunobu very simply: "I was nauseated." He adds: "It was only through Gaugin that I began to appreciate the qualities of *ukiyoe*, and I still feel closer to Gaugin than to *ukiyoe*." His comment that although he likes Sharaku's portraits he likes them as paintings rather than as woodcuts brings to mind a statement by Dr. Fujikake that traditional *ukiyoe* was patterned after the brush, whereas modern

54

creative prints show that their origin is in the carving tool and not the brush.

Saito was reared in the north and came to Tokyo when he was about twenty-five. He was determined to be an artist, but he never found the right teacher and ended up teaching himself. "I've always done the kind of work I want to," he says. "Some people say my art is too earthy, that it 'smells of earth.' Others say it's too posterish. Maybe they're both right and maybe neither is. I can't be bothered, because I'm doing what I want to do."

Still others accuse Saito of catering to American taste. This he denies, but he is emphatic when he goes on to say that the present popularity of creative *hanga* is largely due to the Americans who came to Japan after the war. "The Japanese still condescend to us," he says, "but it was even worse before Komai and I won prizes at the Brazil show in 1951." He is referring to the First Biennial Exhibition of the Modern Art Museum of Sao Paulo. The Japanese submissions to that show arrived late, after the judging had been completed. To compensate, the local Japanese-Brazilian community raised funds so that the exhibition jury could award a couple of prizes to the Japanese. The Japanese art world was rocked when the jury passed up the oil paintings and sculpture to award both prizes to *hanga,* an etching by Tetsuro Komai and a print by Saito (*Staring,* print 29).

Like Munch, and perhaps more so because of his liking for Munch, Saito is strongly influenced by his home country. This is most easily seen in his early prints of winter in Aizu. These black and white prints, clearly descended from Japanese ink painting, were made in 1941, after a nostalgic visit to the scenes of his childhood.

About four years ago he began a series of prints based on the ancient burial figures called *haniwa* ("They have a beauty like nudes," he says), and recently his work has been dominated by scenes around Japan's old capital, Kyoto. He says that these latter prints came about because his study of Mondrian got him interested in Japanese screens. He went to Kyoto to study screens and while there he made the sketches of the Katsura Imperial Villa which resulted in the first of these prints, *Shoji* (print 33). Mondrian's influence is obvious, but this was a phase leading to greater freedom and bolder design.

Being self-taught, Saito evolved an unusual technique of making a color print from a single block. *Alone* (print 34) is a good example. It began with a solid block of *katsura*. Spurning the usual chisels of the woodcut artist, Saito went to work with a *kiri,* a simple tool which resembles an ice pick except that the handle is longer and the steel is shorter and angular instead of round. A Japanese carpenter, rotating the *kiri* rapidly between his palms, will use it to drill small holes to set nails or screws. Saito uses it as his principal carving tool, and with it he scratches or digs at the wood rather than chiseling it.

He cut his block freehand. Saito lays great stress on the ability to draw and sketch, but once the design for *Alone* was determined he set it aside, and neither pasted it to his block nor transferred it by tracing. Nor was his sketch in color. As with many wood-block artists, the ultimate color scheme worked itself out in his mind while he was carving.

Every feature of the print was carved on this one block. In some of his later work, when the influence of Gauguin was strongest and bold masses predominated, Saito would leave some lines uncarved, as for instance between the hair and the background. He would simply paint his colors on the smooth block as one would if one were making a lithograph. But that technique was to come later; for this particular print Saito created a portrait in wood relief.

Although he had reduced to one the many blocks needed for color printing, still he could print with only a single color at a time. He started with the grey of the face. To get the depth of tone he wanted he had to make about ten impressions of the same color. Because his block had no *kento,* once the paper was applied it could never be completely removed until the print was finished; so as he worked on the face he held the paper in place by weights elsewhere on the block. When he had achieved the basic tone he wanted in the face he went on to do the lips and other features, using a darker grey.

The flowers gave him as much trouble as the face. It took a lot of paint and strong pressure to get the quality of color he wanted,

56

and he put aside his *baren* and used his thumb to force the paper deep into the carving of the block. The black of the hair also required several impressions, as did the blue background, which came last. It took him at least half a day to make one print.

This print, with its shading and complex textures, illustrates Saito's early rejection of the emphatic line of *ukiyoe*. Today he finds that line more appealing, but even though he uses simple forms he still tries for elaborate textural effects. Saito himself divides his work into three periods. His early period is dominated by the Aizu snow scenes. Beginning in 1945 he entered a period of realism typified by the portrait just discussed, the portrait of his daughter *Naoko* (print 32), *Venus, The Back Streets of the City,* and *Child of Aizu.* By 1950 a move toward simplification was apparent in such prints as *Staring* (print 29), *Buddhist Statue* (print 31), and his first great cat print, also called *Staring.* This tendency was formally announced, so to speak, in his first one-man show at Mitsukoshi in 1951 and has been gathering speed ever since, as evidenced by his *haniwa* prints (see print 35) and *Shoji* (print 33).

As his style simplified he changed his technique to meet new problems. For his current prints he uses several blocks, made from plywood and cut with flat chisels. He usually uses ply faced with *katsura, rawan, yanagi,* or *keyaki,* depending on the type of cutting and the final effect he wants. *Keyaki,* for example, has a broad, handsome longitudinal grain, and he uses it when he wants such a grain in his design.

Saito did a good deal of research to find the best paper for his prints. He ended up with *kizuki hosho,* the same great paper used for most *ukiyoe.* A handmade paper of the *kozo* family, it is usually characterized by parallel lines like watermarks caused by the threads which act like a woof in holding together the screen of tiny bamboo strips with which the paper is made. Saito orders his paper specially to get it without these lines. Usually he gets it already sized with animal glue, but to achieve the soft effect of his Aizu snow prints he uses the same paper without sizing.

Internationally exhibited, internationally admired, and internationally purchased, Saito is an artist who has arrived. This is not to say that he has solidified into a style, for his tempo of development was never faster, the vitality with which he assimilates new ideas was never greater, than it is today. He is the kind of artist who gives the contemporary collector both pleasures and problems—an exciting career to trace, but an agonizing choice in trying to pick the best from each new show.

Early in 1956 Saito left for a visit in the United States. The new perspective and fresh look that this trip will give him will certainly show in his work. Just how it will show one can only guess, but an artist as vigorous and forthright as Saito should find much in America to stimulate him, and one looks forward to the new prints which will follow.

29. *Staring (1950)*　　　　　　　　　　　　KIYOSHI SAITO

KIYOSHI
SAITO

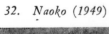

30. *Winter in Aizu (1941)*

31. *Buddhist Statue (1950)*

32. *Naoko (1949)*

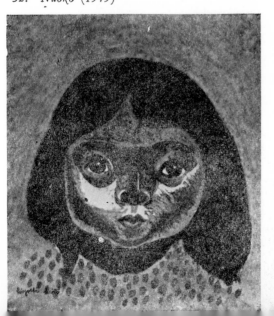

33. *Shoji (1954)*

KIYOSHI SAITO

34. *Alone*
(1947)

35. *Earthenware and Haniwa* (1952)

KIYOSHI
SAITO

36. *All Cats Are Grey at Night* (1952)

JUN'ICHIRO SEKINO

JUN'ICHIRO SEKINO (BORN 1914) PRESENTS A contrast to Saito in many ways. There is a good deal more of the artisan in Sekino, and while Saito deplores the drudgery of print-making, Sekino likes it. Saito will discuss at length the artists who have influenced him and point out in his own work the effects of their influence. Sekino's artistic heredity is more difficult to trace.

Like Saito, he is largely self-taught, although he did attend a small private art school where he worked in oil, doing academic studies of nudes and very ordinary landscapes. He says he has always liked Sharaku and has had periods of liking Hiroshige, Lautrec, Rembrandt, and Anders Zorn, the Swedish etcher and oil painter. "But more than these men," he says, "I think my work

63

has been influenced by Dürer. One of the things I like most about him is his thoroughness, his corner-to-corner completeness." Finally, as Sekino became interested in woodprints he came under the influence of Onchi, as his portraits clearly show.

Sekino's work is not, however, so much influenced by conscious study of other artists as by the natural exposure to the currents of his time and place. He would much rather talk about subject matter than style—such direct and personal things as his strong sense of fate and the loneliness of life, and the beauty of his children growing up. At the risk of a generalization, it can be said that where Saito's approach is intellectual, Sekino's is emotional.

It may be this which draws Sekino to the theatre. Certainly he has made the finest theatrical prints of our day: a wonderfully satisfying portrait of Kichiemon Nakamura (print 38), the doyen of Kabuki actors until his death in 1954, and several fine studies of Bunraku, Japan's unique puppet theatre.

"During the war the theatres were mostly closed," says Sekino, "but the actors often performed for the troops or workers. I got to know Kichiemon by a stroke of good luck: he brought his Kabuki company to entertain at the factory where I'd been mobilized, and the foreman appointed me to look after them while they were there." This was the start of an acquaintance which developed through a mutual enthusiasm for *haiku,* the classical Japanese seventeen-syllable verse form. After the war Sekino edited a modern collection of these poems, and Kichiemon, who painted and wrote poetry in the Kabuki tradition of versatility, became a contributor. Sekino made his sketches for the portrait during his visits in connection with the *haiku* book.

Sekino, who like most of the rest of the workers was never quite sure what his factory was producing, was also appointed to take care of the Bunraku artists when the puppet theatre came to boost morale. Sketches he made after that introduction are still resulting in prints, among them the dramatic portrait of the grand old man of the company, Bungoro, and the later portraits of Eizo (print 40) and Monjuro (print 41).

Since editing the collection of *haiku* in 1945 Sekino has concentrated

64

on his *hanga* and has been able to make a living from his prints and the usual concomitants of illustration and book design.

Because he taught himself technique from books written by skilled artisans, his technique is conservative. He starts with a fairly complete sketch, which he transfers to the blocks by carbon paper or mimeograph stencils. His final print is usually very close to his original idea.

He carves with the traditional chisels, and like a good workman he keeps them very sharp. The facial shadings of his portraits are achieved by shallow, beveled cuts with a wide, curved chisel.

He uses plywood for most of his blocks, but he falls back on a block of solid *katsura* when he needs sharp definition. For example, *Eizo and Matsuomaru* (print 40) was made with six blocks of plywood faced with firm, close-grained *shina* and one solid block of *katsura* on which he carved the fine details of the faces. For prints other than portraits he frequently uses plywood faced with *rawan,* which has a coarse, even grain. He gets an interesting textural effect with this wood by scouring out the soft part of the grain with a wire brush. A block so treated yields a print with even, parallel unprinted streaks. Sometimes he crosses two such blocks to obtain crosshatching, a trick much the same as that used by traditional *ukiyoe* artisans when they achieved the amazingly fine detail of mosquito netting by carving the vertical lines on one block and the horizontal lines on another.

He prints on *torinoko* paper. He sizes his own paper with animal glue, hangs it up to dry, and moistens it again before printing, all in the traditional way. His editions are from twenty to fifty, but he usually attempts to print only three at a time and commonly finds that only two of these will turn out to be satisfactory.

Sekino lives in one of Tokyo's myriad little off-the-avenue residential areas, laced by unnamed, unpaved lanes and punctuated by the neighborhood bathhouse. His studio is upstairs, and when he comes down, the visitor's first impression is of big wide eyes and a huge shock of unruly black hair. Ingenuous and friendly, he consistently manages to give the impression of fresh pleasure with the world, but nothing makes him light up like consideration of his three extraordinarily handsome and winning children, two boys and a girl, who have often appeared in his prints (see prints 37, 42, and 43). Although portraits are his most distinctive and forceful work, they do not monopolize his output. His early prints are chiefly genre pieces reflecting the life of the northern province where he grew up, and his later work includes landscapes and still lifes, such as the striking *Aquarium* (print 39). He also does etchings and lithographs, most of which are surrealistic.

Working in all three media has made him conscious that each has its own potential, that a woodprint should not compete with a lithograph or a brush painting but should exploit the special possibilities inherent in wood. In his words, "the chisel has its own taste."

This accounts for his sharp swing away from the shadows and shadings of painting and toward the sharp, clear lines which have characterized woodprints in the past. In *A Boy and His Rooster* (print 42) he has moved so far as to eliminate characterization: this is less a portrait than pictorial design. It is the same simplification of form which marks the recent work of Saito and some of the others, but Sekino couldn't recall that they had ever discussed it together. "I think it's just a natural development in making prints," he says.

In this way he has faced up to the problem of simplifying his design to meet the demands of his medium without losing the emotional charge of his idea. It is not a new problem nor one unique to Sekino, but it is perhaps revealed more clearly in him than it is in most artists, and it is an absorbing study to trace his progress as he pares away the nonessentials of style to get at the core of feeling. As print follows print his growing success reveals an intuitive artist, increasingly the master of wood and chisel and *baren,* but still warm, human, and close to the heart.

37. My Daughter (1952)　　　　　　　　JUN'ICHIRO SEKINO

38. *Kichiemon, Kabuki Actor* (1947)

39. *Aquarium* (1947)

40. *Eizo and Matsuomaru* (1953)

JUN'ICHIRO SEKINO

41. *Monjuro and Jihei* (1954)

JUN'ICHIRO
SEKINO

42. *A Boy and His Rooster (1954)*

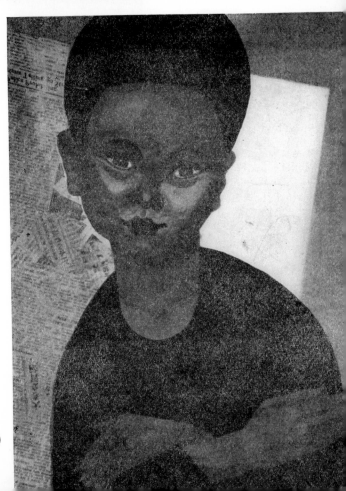

43. *My Son (1952)*

8
TAKUMI
SHINAGAWA

OF ALL THESE ARTISTS TAKUMI SHINAGAWA (born 1907) is probably the most varied in output. Tall, slim, and poised, with a wide forehead and a tapering face, his lively eyes reflect a questioning intelligence. Techniques fascinate him, and he continually experiments. In his prints he moves from wood blocks to paper blocks and back again, but his activity is not limited to prints: his studio is hung with mobiles, which he makes from wire and colored plastic; he creates faces, figures, and abstract forms in paper, metal, and wire; and he is an ingenious, often spectacular, photographer in both black and white and color. He used to do his own camera work, but during the war, he says, "I ate my camera." Now he collaborates with a commercial photographer, and their

71

efforts often appear as commercial art. In addition to all this, he takes an occasional fling at teaching and frequently contributes articles on *hanga* technique to textbooks and magazines.

Often work in one medium suggests another. To illustrate, Shinagawa points to a mobile hanging in his studio, a spiral form cut from plastic. He liked this form so well that he made an abstract print based on the same idea. Then he created the shape in wire. The next step was a carefully designed photograph of the wire figure, and in the photograph he found that the shadow cast by the wire suggested an entirely new form. He is still exploring the possibilities.

This restless experimentation may cause one to wonder whether Shinagawa will ever apply himself to one medium long enough to realize his full potential, but there is no doubt that his inquiring mind has probed some questions very deeply.

He says: "When I was beginning to make woodprints, I got hold of a fragment of *ukiyoe*. The more I studied it the more I was struck by the depth of color in that print. When I held it up against the light it looked like stained glass. I realized then that a good print is much more than color laid on paper. The paint has to go into the paper, to become part of the paper. Often the pigments should be mixed in the paper by applying one over another to get a living, glowing color deep in the paper. I was excited by my discoveries and I spoke to Dr. Fujikake about it. He confirmed my thinking and went on to say that fakes of old prints may often be detected by lack of depth in the color."

Shinagawa compares the quality of color in prints with the quality of color in certain old tapestries which he saw in a recent exhibition loaned by the Louvre, pointing out that the subdued tones of the tapestry are quite different from the bright hues of the individual threads. To clinch this point he shows two samples of the same paint, first when it is brushed on paper, and second when it is printed on the same paper with a wood block. The difference in tone is astounding. As might be expected, his exploration of the subject has made Shinagawa very particular about his paints, and he mixes his own, often using European pigments.

72

He feels just as intensely about the line of *ukiyoe,* the "singing line" as Michener has called it. "The figures of *ukiyoe* are distorted," he will say. "Of course, we all know that. But why?" And he will answer his own question: "Because they were carved in wood. The wood modifies the line as it modifies the color."

Shinagawa has tried different approaches to the problem of line. In his monocolor prints he developed the idea of cutting away the line to reveal the form behind it. "My father-in-law was a wood sculptor," Shinagawa says, "a classical Buddhist wood sculptor, and I found myself fascinated by the idea of what he had cut away in creating the form that was left. This was the idea in my mind when I was making my monocolor prints, to cut away the line to reveal the form and its shadows."

In his abstract prints Shinagawa has developed another way of creating a line. For example, he will print red on top of yellow. Where he has cut away the red block, a line of yellow remains.

"Let me explain it this way," Shinagawa says. "If I draw or visualize a line on a block and then cut away the wood on both sides to leave that line, I feel that I am merely reproducing a line I previously created. But if I take my chisel and gouge out the line, I feel that my hand and my mind are working together in an act of creation, the same way as a painter with a brush. It's an entirely different kind of feeling, spontaneous and free."

Shinagawa sums up by saying that he is attempting to realize in the modern idiom the essence of traditional *ukiyoe* as a woodprint. He is trying to give modern expression to what he considers the basic fundamentals of the woodprint, the qualities of line and color which are unique to the use of wood and which were lost when *ukiyoe* slipped from greatness to become a process of mere reproduction.

Subject matter is something else again. "Nobody in my house wears kimono," he says. "It would be ridiculous for me to make pictures of kimonoed beauties. Japanese art can't stay aloof from world currents, but that doesn't make a Japanese artist any less Japanese. And I certainly don't agree that, in becoming universal, Japanese art has become degraded."

Speaking of his own development as an artist, Shinagawa says that to do something modern an artist must go through cubism. He has always been interested in abstract art, and while the observer who has followed his exhibitions would trace a marked change from his earlier realistic work to his present abstract prints, he says this is misleading. His own interests have not changed he says, only the sort of thing he has done for exhibition.

He acknowledges the influence of Onchi; he feels some kinship to Miro; he admires Picasso. He was particularly impressed by Picasso's lithographs in a recent exhibition of lithographs by foreign artists. "Picasso was the only one who was exploiting the lithograph," he says. "The others all looked like lithographic reproductions, but Picasso had used the unique qualities of the lithographic process to create something which could not have been done in any other medium. That is what a woodcut artist must do when he makes a woodcut."

Shinagawa went to the Tokyo metropolitan technical school in Tsukiji, where he studied a wide range of handicrafts. Although he first had ideas of becoming an oil painter, he was an avid experimenter in paper and wire. A friend suggested it would be interesting to show some of this work to Onchi, and he did, together with one woodblock print which he made. Onchi's encouragement really started him making prints.

Like Onchi, Shinagawa has experimented widely with paper blocks, and many of his prints are made with paper blocks or a combination of wood and paper blocks. He is particularly interested in the textural effects he can obtain by making blocks from different papers. For example, a paper of uneven thickness will give a mottled effect. In printing from paper blocks Shinagawa usually fastens the blocks to a board and prints the same way he would from a wood block, using a *kento* on the board. If he wants a lighter effect he may lay the print on its back, place the paper block on top, and print with a thin paper between the block and his *baren*.

Shinagawa usually limits his editions to about twenty, but in printing from paper blocks he can make only four prints at a time

74

44. *Kabuki Actor (1953)*   TAKUMI SHINAGAWA

because the blocks swell so rapidly and must be put away to dry before they can be used again. Of course the same problem is common to wood blocks but to a much lesser degree: a printer can get about two hundred impressions from *sakura* blocks before the swelling destroys the registry.

For his wood blocks he uses plywood, faced with *shina* for his shallow-cut monocolor prints and with *rawan* when he is cutting bold masses. When he was carving his monocolor prints he used a very shallow, beveled cut made with a wide, curved chisel and a flat chisel with a curved edge. From his father-in-law he has inherited both a remarkable collection of knives and chisels, many of a kind and quality no longer available, and his studio, still redolent of a sculptor's work with its plaster casts and unfinished wood carvings.

In some of his prints Shinagawa uses a form of embossing achieved by hard pressure with the *baren* over cuts in the wood made with the *kiri,* the same sharp-pointed carpenter's tool that Saito uses for so much of his work. Shinagawa may emboss the whole surface of other prints by placing a sheet of sandpaper behind his paper while he prints.

He prints on *torinoko* paper. Often he gives it additional thickness by pasting a sheet of thin, tough tissue on the back. He sizes his own paper.

Among his noteworthy prints are *Stone Buddha* (print 45), which catches the feeling of lush jungle decay in tones of green and yellow; *Cloud* (print 47), *Light,* and *Vision by the Sea,* all from the period when he was working with shallow-carved blocks in tones of brown; and, more recently, *Face on the Body* (print 49), *Kabuki Actor* (print 44), *Devil Tile* (print 48), and *Ghost Story* (print 50). With Shinagawa's approach, his deep involvement in technique, and his inquisitive search for new methods, it is hard to guess what line his future work will take, but it certainly will not be dull. There is no room for dullness in a mind that questions so ceaselessly.

45. *Stone Buddha* (1947)

TAKUMI
SHINAGAWA

46. *Concaves (1951)*

47. *Cloud*
(1949)

TAKUMI
SHINAGAWA

48. *Devil*
Tile (1954)

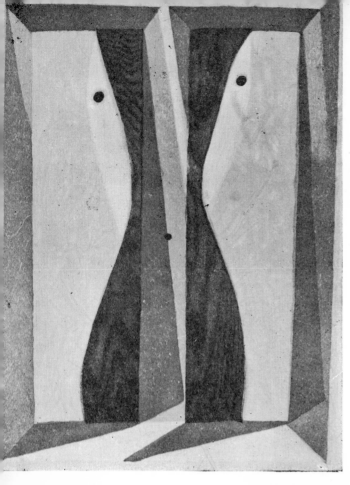

49. *Face on the Body (1952)*

TAKUMI
SHINAGAWA

50   *Ghost Story (1955)*

9
SHIKO
MUNAKATA

IF SHIKO MUNAKATA (BORN 1903) BELONGS to the *hanga* school, he is a rebel among rebels. It seems much more likely, however, that the accident of contemporaneity has thrown him into an association with the other artists which is comfortable for neither side. As Robert T. Paine, Jr., has said: "It is a question whether he is not more indebted to the medieval prints of Buddhist deities in black and white than he is to any modern adventure in making the limited area of a book page or print visually exciting."

The medieval prints of which Paine speaks are those already mentioned in the discussion of Hiratsuka. The similarities between these prints and Munakata's work are apparent, and Munakata himself is first to claim the kinship. Like the early prints, Munakata's work is basically religious, dominated by Buddhist themes which he finds deep and profound, and in technique limited to single-block prints in black and white, though he sometimes adds tints of other colors with a brush.

"Other artists work in black and white," says Munakata, "but in my prints the relationship of the two colors is peculiarly and inherently Japanese." Here, in Munakata's complete rejection of foreign influences, is probably the most obvious point of difference with the other artists. He speaks of his formula of beauty in dimensional terms: "When an artist strives for universality, for the width of universal appreciation, he ends up without depth, with only the superficial aspects of beauty. I don't want to be universal. I deplore alien borrowings. I want my work to be purely Japanese." And he goes on: "My work is based on Zen Buddhism. Others treat black as black ink. To me it is life itself."

Munakata even writes the word *hanga* differently. From the dozens of characters which could be read to give the same sounds, the commonly accepted choice (版画) may be translated as "print picture," but Munakata uses characters (板画) which translate as "board picture." He makes much of the distinction, pointing out that his way of writing emphasizes the basic materials from which the picture is made, while the other characters emphasize the process and hence the artist.

This renunciation of self is a firm tenet of Zen art. Langdon Warner illuminated the whole idea in his book *The Enduring Art of Japan,* when he wrote: "Zen artists discovered that the principle of *muga* (it is not I that am doing this) opens the gate for the necessary essential truth to flow in. When the self does not control the drawing, meaning must. This principle runs all through Zen teachings, especially where action is involved. It is related to the Taoist mistrust of the human intervention which clogs the channels of the Way."

Says Munakata: "Too many artists have too much of self in their work. Any self-conscious effort to create something beautiful can only be a pretense, and a craving for recognition can lead to nothing good. True art must be pure and simple. Maybe we have to go back to the ancient Buddhist prints for the real art of the wood block. They were carved by artisans, not artists. They weren't trying to make a name for themselves. Their work is pure."

Artists being artists and also human, such jibes do not go unanswered. A fellow artist has said that Munakata is less an artist than a religious sect. "There's a word for him," he went on. "He's *kamigakari*—obsessed with God."

Openly scornful as he is of the work of most of his contemporaries, it is easy to understand why Munakata is not a member of the *Hanga* Association. Instead he is closely associated with the *mingei* folkcraft group, where his religiosity and his dedication to things Japanese is less out of place. One of the leaders of that group, the potter Kanjiro Kawai, has said that he's the greatest Japanese artist since Tessai Tomioka (1836–1924), adding that maybe he's greater than Tessai.

This is a remark that surely must have pleased Munakata, who is a fervent admirer of Tessai's powerful brush. Though the influence of Tessai is obvious, Munakata's taste in Japanese art is catholic: he likes Shubun, Sesshu, Sotatsu, Korin, and Taiga; the story picture scrolls of the Kamakura period (1185–1392); the sumptuous screens of the Momoyama period (1568–1615); and the *ukiyoe* artists, of whom he says "they were all great—there is something to admire in each of them." In European art his favorite, understandably, is van Gogh; less understandably he also names Chavannes.

Munakata sketches his career in this way: "I started out to be an oil painter. I won a lot of prizes and people thought I was successful, but as I went along I realized I could never be a Picasso. For European artists, oil is their heritage, but it wasn't mine. I wanted the universe at the tip of my brush and I realized it never could be while I worked in a borrowed medium. I looked back to my own country, back to Japan, and I saw that the medium in my heritage was the woodblock print.

"As I developed I found a simple approach, and at first I was satisfied. Then I found I was taking my work too lightly. I was too facile. I had to suffer a little. I had to get the spirit of life in my carving tool.

"After twenty years of work I'm beginning to get it. Up to now my work has depended on my conscious power. Now when I work, the tool doesn't follow my mind. The mind itself goes, and the tool walks alone. Only when that happens can art be genuine."

Munakata is no mild-mannered advocate. As he talks his voice becomes loud, words tumble out one after another in a compulsive crescendo, and his whole body tenses and springs in great gestures. He is a stocky, rumpled dynamo of a man, nearsightedly peering at a world he cannot quite make out, wanting to be great good friends with it but ready if necessary to take it on in a fiery and articulate defense of his creed.

His work is as explosive as his personality. At its best it is a great, triumphant surge of sheer vitality, at its worst it is uncontrolled frenzy.

Despite his insistence that only now is he "beginning to get it," his early prints include many of his best. In 1937 he produced the twenty-three prints of the *Kegon Series,* one of which is *The Deity of the Wind* (print 52). "These were my first Buddhist prints," he says, "and they set me on my career. People have identified them with the Kegon Sutra, but they really have no connection. I just wanted to give them a grand name." He followed in 1938 with two memorable series, a set of thirty-one prints based on the Noh drama *Uto,* from which *Sand Nest* (print 56) is taken, and the thirty-five prints suggested by the Kannon Sutra, among them *Magora* (print 53). In 1939 came the massive figures of the *Ten Great Disciples of Buddha,* including *Ragora* (print 51). All this, however, is not to deny his impressive later work like *The Garden* (print 54), *Hisatsu* (print 57), *Hawk Woman* (print 55), and the big, dynamic *The Hunters.*

Because he was shown briefly in a United States Information Service film on the arts of Japan, probably more people have seen Munakata at work than any of the other artists discussed here. They have seen him lean close to the board with a concentration intensified by his nearsightedness, and they have watched in fascination as he daubs a few lines on a board and then attacks it in a furious out-

51. Ragora (1937)   SHIKO MUNAKATA

burst of speed that sends chips flying. Those who have seen can understand his saying that "the mind goes, and the tool walks alone." Only intuition could guide such violent activity.

"In carving," says Munakata, "I aim to take a board and make it live," so he makes use of the whole board. His figure touches or goes off the board at top and bottom and both sides, and he usually leaves the corners so they will print and demonstrate that the entire board was used.

For small prints he makes a drawing on paper, which he pastes on the board, but for large prints he draws directly on the board. In either case the drawing consists of the roughest kind of notation, a sort of shorthand reference to what Munakata calls "the monster," a happy epithet for his conception of the print.

He uses a straight chisel for hard lines and a curved chisel for softer ones. He holds his chisel like a brush or pencil and turns the block as he works. His blocks are solid *katsura*. "The choice of wood shows the character of the artist," he says. "*Ho* spreads as you cut it so that the chisel runs easily. *Katsura* is tougher and as it's cut it pinches the tool, so that it gives me some resistance."

Munakata prints on thin, unsized *kozo* paper, usually *etchu* from Toyama or *izumo* from Shimane. Since his entire block is carved, there is no place for a *kento,* and once on the block the paper is left there until the print is complete, one portion at a time being lifted to check the depth of color.

For his black he uses ordinary *sumi,* "the cheapest I can get." He does not try for the intense black of Hiratsuka but rather for a variety of tone. When he tints his prints he brushes color on the back and lets it seep through, pointing out that color seeping into paper is a special quality of *hanga.* To get the misty effect he sometimes uses he moistens his paper before printing.

Munakata may not strive for universal appreciation, but he was a happy man—and deservedly so—when he won first prize for *hanga* at Sao Paulo's 1955 international show. The prize-winning work was a panel of three great figures with *Ragora* (print 51) in the middle. In congratulating him a friend laughingly remarked that the honor made him thoroughly eligible for the attacks which young artists direct toward their successful elders. Munakata was delighted with the thought. "Good!" he exclaimed. "That's the way it should be. Tear down the old to make way for the new!"

A man as exuberantly vital as Munakata is inevitably thinking of new, big things. Though he has made some large prints, usually by pasting smaller sections together, he plans to go still further, and visualizes prints which will stretch the full length of his long studio. In this connection he is toying with another idea. "Up to now I have done Buddhist motifs through nudes of Orientals, because Oriental figures are small and pleasant. For these enormous prints, these prints on a grand scale, I think that I should use Western nudes. But," he concludes, "regardless of size or scope, one thing is certain: my work must be not of the mind, not of the finger-tips, but of the heart."

84

52. *The Deity of the Wind* (1937)

SHIKO MUNAKATA

53. *Magora* (1938)

54. The Garden
(1950)

SHIKO
MUNAKATA

55. Hawk
Woman (1955)

56. *Sand Nest* (1938)

SHIKO
MUNAKATA

57. *Hisatsu* (1954)

10
ON THE
SIDE

Sumio Kawakami
Takeo Takei
Shigeru Hatsuyama

NOT ALL ARTISTS LIVE IN THE VORTEX OF A MOVEMENT. SOME CHOOSE THE edges, working in their own special way, not too much concerned about what others may be doing. Often the work of such men has a particular interest because it develops along personal and unique lines.

Sumio Kawakami, Takeo Takei, and Shigeru Hatsuyama are three men who have had solid, satisfying professions. They have turned to prints for creative expression, and in each case the results are sharply individual. Because prints are consciously an avocation with them, they have been able to develop distinctively, free from the pressures and preoccupations that tend to mold the full-time artist whether he seeks a congenial group or tries to stand apart.

These three are knowing, sophisticated artists, although they came by their educations quite differently. Their sufficiency and self-assurance shows in their prints, which may sometimes reveal a similarity of intent with other artists, but demonstrate as well that there has been no superficial borrowing. Part-time artists though

89

they are, their work commands attention and respect for its individuality, its stability, and its charm.

SUMIO KAWAKAMI

The prints of Sumio Kawakami (born 1895) are brisk pictorial footnotes to history, a lively look at what happened when the somewhat reluctant Japanese confronted the Western world. This is a subject which has fascinated both scholar and satirist, and Kawakami makes good use of the wealth of material.

The West's more recent and telling intrusion was inaugurated by Commodore Perry only a century ago, but two hundred and fifty years before that the Portuguese and Dutch were jockeying for trade at Nagasaki. This was an ingression the wary Japanese kept under strict control, and finally restricted to a tiny beachhead, but it was there, and its effect was not limited to the introduction of sponge cake and *tempura* (seafood and vegetables dipped in batter and cooked in oil), great though these blessings are. Kawakami's excursions into this period are usually referred to as *namban* prints, but he points out that *namban* (people from the south, a term inherited from the Chinese) refers specifically to the Portuguese and Spanish; that another word, *komo* (red-headed people), was used for the Dutch; and that his prints deal as much with the Dutch as with the Portuguese. It is also clear that, regardless of subject matter, his is not *namban* art, nor is it intended to be.

Kawakami's background provides the key to his preoccupation with the foreigner's impact on Japan. He was born in Yokohama, which, together with Kobe and Nagasaki, was then one of the great points of contact; he attended a mission school, where again he watched the two cultures battling it out; and his father was an extraordinary gentleman who spent all his life promoting the

90

modernism of the West in a career which ranged from journalism to the manufacture of medicines.

After Kawakami had finished college at Aoyama Gakuin in Tokyo his father summoned him and told him to go to America. "Why?" asked Kawakami. "For any reason you like," was the answer. "You won't starve, and I want you to have the experience."

He moved in with family friends near Seattle and, looking about for something to do, decided that house painting might be a good idea. After a brief trial, however, the house painters with whom he worked advised him that he just didn't seem to be cut out for that trade, and added that if he felt he must paint, he would do better to turn to art. Although he had always liked art and had even made a few woodblocks while in middle school, he had never had any training in art nor thought of becoming an artist, and this advice startled him. While digesting it he took a job in Alaska canning fish. Three or four months later he had about decided to go to a commercial-art school in Chicago to learn window display, when a younger brother died and he returned to Tokyo. After a term with an export firm he moved to Utsunomiya, north of Tokyo, and began to teach English, a career he has held to for almost thirty years.

At about the same time he resumed his interest in art as an avocation. He started submitting drawings to a literary magazine which solicited such contributions (Hiratsuka was doing the same thing and they met in this way), and he started seriously to make prints. He exhibited with the *Hanga* Association as early as their second show.

Kawakami draws many ideas from his own large collection of the old books with which the Japanese nation first tackled Western languages and ideas. One of these, *The Standard First Reader for Beginners* by Epes Sargent, published in America in 1866, was laboriously reproduced by woodblock: with no metal type at their disposal, the Japanese cut a *sakura* block for every page, faithfully copying each word and picture. Another, Barnes' *New National Reader* of 1883, was reproduced by the engraving process. An even richer source of material are the texts published by the Education Ministry in the early 1870's, in which the picture of a thing is combined with the German, English, and French words for it, all done by woodblock. These old illustrations not only show contemporary costumes, accoutrements, and vehicles, but give an insight into what the Japanese found most engrossing in the new world that was opening up to them. They also provide occasional amusement, as when "school playground" is translated into Japanese as "digestive area."

Digging back into the earlier invasion by the West, Kawakami has uncovered many curious facts. He thinks it may come as a shock to some Japanese to learn that their great general Hideyoshi (1536–1598) slept in a brass bed, of which he installed several in Osaka castle. Tobacco was also introduced to Japan about the same time, and old pipes are another of Kawakami's hobbies. "Some of the big ones had a dual purpose," he notes. "They were designed to be used as weapons if the need arose." Both beds and pipes are given the Kawakami treatment in one of his recent prints, *Nambanesque Behavior* (print 60).

This print, like almost all of his prints for the past twenty years, was made from a single block and then colored by hand. "I used to make landscapes in multi-block color prints," he says, "but people are what I'm really interested in, and ever since I switched to the *namban* prints I've brushed on my color." This seems a perfectly logical method for Kawakami because he is primarily interested in the narrative quality which is conveyed by his line block, and color is merely an accessory element.

The literary influence in his work is obvious. He is absorbed in historical subject matter, but his prints emerge as art, strongly composed and well organized, witty and charming. Some of the best include *Map of the Heart, Women and Lamps, When the Moon Comes Out,* and *Arrival of a Portuguese Ship* (print 59).

The same literary influence that dominates his prints is also reflected in the poetry he somehow finds time to write, and in the fact that he is more interested in making books than single prints. "I've never counted my books," he says, "but I think I was the first to make them, and I've made at least one a year, often more. Incidentally, it's always been easy to sell the usual edition of fifty books, but hard to sell single prints. Before the war I could have lived on the proceeds of two books a year, and adding that to my teacher's salary, I made more than the principal. Unfortunately, the price of books and art hasn't risen proportionately to rent and the price of rice, and to make a living now I'd have to turn out a book a month."

To help him make his books, which include text as well as pictures, Kawakami has carved about eight hundred ideographs on individual small blocks of *sakura*. He sets these up like movable type in a wooden frame and then prints from them with a *baren*. Since he frequently uses a text three or four hundred years old, or simulates such language himself, many of his characters are archaic and force his readers to their dictionaries.

Today Kawakami is very grey, round-faced, and a little heavy. He has difficulty walking, so he lives close to his school. "I was never much in the swim of things as far as prints were concerned," he says. "Since I didn't live in Tokyo I never knew many of the print artists and never was much influenced by them. I've just gone my own way, doing what interested me, and hoping it would interest somebody else. If it has, I'm happy."

The names of Takeo Takei and Shigeru Hatsuyama are linked as Japan's two leading illustrators of children's books. Takei (born 1894) entered that field thirty-five years ago, just after graduating from the government art academy at Ueno. He has made his living that way ever since, but as he says: *"Hanga* is more than a hobby with me: I put too much time and effort in my prints to think of them that way."

Takei's most personal creations are a series of miniature books into which he

TAKEO TAKEI

93

has poured his skill and imagination for twenty years. The series started with a volume published in 1935, and issues have appeared at irregular intervals ever since, slowed by the war, but accelerated of late. At this writing the twenty-eighth of the series has been published, and several more are in the planning stage.

The first four books were printed by letter press from zinc plates, but with the fifth book Takei started to make the books by *hanga*. His subjects have ranged from *kokeshi* dolls and playing cards to the beggars of Japan and the life of St. Agnes, and his methods have the same variety, for since the fifth book he has tried to use a different technique for each volume. He admits he hasn't quite succeeded in this aim, but considering the length of the series he has done remarkably well, and he has invented a number of new processes in the attempt.

In addition to the common techniques of woodblock, wood engraving, stencil, etching, and lithograph, some of his more unusual techniques are as follows:

1. Scratch-board. This process is somewhat similar to dry-point engraving, except that for a plate one uses a sheet of celluloid coated with paint. The picture is scratched in this paint with a needle, and the plate is then used as a negative from which a metal plate is made for printing. Book six was made this way.

2. Vari-type. This is a process invented and named by Takei. Color is brushed on a smooth block, and the paper to be printed is laid on this block. On top of the paper Takei places a precise little paper form, cut out and pasted in different thicknesses and different textures. On top of this form goes another sheet of paper, usually newspaper, so he can use his *baren*. The paper form causes an uneven pressure on the printing surface, and the result is a soft image of the form. Takei used this process in his twentieth book.

3. An unusual method of rubbing. Takei first carves a bas-relief in clay, from which he makes a clay negative, from which he makes a plaster positive, from which he makes another negative in copper electroplate, from which he makes a rubbing. Book twenty-one was born this way.

4. Clay blocks. Takei carves clay blocks, later fired at the kilns

in Seto. This process borrows something from the technique of clay seals: he uses the kind of paste ink used with seals, tamping it on the block rather than brushing it, but he prints from the block with a *baren* as though it were a wood block. Takei made book twenty-three this way and used an improved version for book twenty-five.

5. Another rubbing technique. "This is a technique no one knows," says Takei. He makes a paper block of varied surface and thickness, sometimes adding other materials like cloth, lace, sandpaper, or bamboo leaf (which has a grooved surface). He prints on thin, soft paper, which is laid on this block. On top of the paper goes carbon paper (good for only one use), then a sheet of newspaper. He prints with a specially prepared *baren,* thin sheets of rubber being inserted under the cover so he can vary the pressure to get very delicate shading. Book twenty-four demonstrates this process.

"Changing processes like this keeps my work from formalizing," says Takei. "It keeps it fresh, and me young."

Takei was born in Nagano and went through middle school there. Unlike most of the other artists of this group, he has an air of courtliness about him, a touch of elegance. His face is rectangular, with a strong jaw line which is becoming a little jowly. Thinning hair is brushed straight back from a high forehead. At Ueno he was one year behind Onchi, but unlike Onchi he was a serious student and went through to graduation. The two had little in common and scarcely knew each other at school. Their long association and friendship began a few years later.

Takei's course at Ueno was oil painting, but he had a brief exposure to etching when students in oil were recruited for a study course in that medium which otherwise would have had no takers. After Ueno he became seriously interested in *hanga,* and, fascinated by the whole concept of printing, he dropped his oil painting completely.

For an early and decisive influence he looks back to the group of artists and writers called Shirakaba and their magazine of the same name, through which he was exposed to the work of Cezanne, van Gogh, and Gauguin. Later he became interested in Paul Klee, and he feels that he has much in common with Klee. "When my prints were shown in America," he says, "some critics cited the influence of Miro, but the fact was that I had never seen a Miro. I've seen some of his work now, but I feel much more akin to Klee."

Prints such as *Devils* (print 61), *Landscape* (print 62), *Still Life*, and *On the Table* show Takei's skill and range, for like Klee he is eternally seeking new means of expression. His years of experience as an illustrator have given him a tremendous technical facility and ease, which enable him to experiment all the more freely. A print like *Devils* readily reveals his familiarity with Klee's work, but it is an influence which has been thoroughly transformed by his own distinctive and Japanese vision.

SHIGERU HATSUYAMA

Shigeru Hatsuyama (born 1897), like Takei one of Japan's most successful artists for children, spent his childhood in Tokyo's rough, tough, and gay Asakusa district. A scar on his thumb is a reminder of his first attempt at carving a block of wood. This pregnant event occurred at about the age of four, when he took a chisel from his carpenter father's tool chest and tried to groove a board. Other than this memory his father seems to have contributed little toward raising his son, and it was his mother who supported the family and brought him up.

"I remember that I started to draw when I was about six," he says, "and it must have made an impression on my mother, because when I was eight she started taking me to a Japanese-style painter for weekly lessons. I was much too young to study art, and since about all my teacher did was give me some of his work to copy, we had a very unsatisfactory year together. I rebelled against copying from him just as I rebelled against the same sort of copywork in my art classes at school. I was given very bad marks in art at school." It was this kind of art instruction by imitation against which Kanae Yamamoto inaugurated his fight several years later.

"I left elementary school when I was about nine," Hatsuyama continues, "and my mother got me a job as an office boy in a light-metal shop. Unfortunately, there were two older office boys who made my life miserable. It was my first taste of society. I ran away.

"Then mother apprenticed me to a shop where they dyed textiles in a variation of the *yuzen* process: paste was applied to the cloth to cover up the portions that were to be left undyed; after dye was brushed on the areas left uncovered, the paste was washed out. I was only ten and had very little to do with the dyeing. Like any young apprentice under the old system, I was pretty much taken into the family as another son. I ran errands, helped around the kitchen, sometimes mixed colors. The shop policy was to train the boys by giving them some of the designer's work to copy in the evening, but I still disliked copying. More than anything else I wanted to draw and paint, but no one at the shop would even look at my drawings. I used to be fascinated by the old armor in curio shops. I had never learned to sketch, but I would stare at a suit of armor until I thought I had memorized every detail, and then in the evenings at the shop I would hunt in magazines for illustrations showing armor and color them from memory.

"This sort of thing used to exasperate the men at the shop. 'What do you want to be,' they would ask, 'an expert dyer or an artist? If you want to be a dyer, learn this work. If you want to be an artist, learn to be a beggar.'

"My apprenticeship was for ten years, but after five I ran away and went back home. Mother went around to apologize for my conduct but I don't think she had meant me for the dyeing trade. I think mostly she wanted me to have the experience of living with other people in a family atmosphere, something I never had at home."

There was a Zen temple near his home, and in the Zen tradition the priest spent a good deal of his spare time making brush drawings.

Young Hatsuyama spent hours watching the priest, who, impressed by the boy, introduced him to a prominent newspaper illustrator, Sengai Ikawa.

"I became Ikawa's student," says Hatsuyama, "and this was something I really worked at. The best training I got was when he was too busy to read the current novel. I'd read it for him and make pencil sketches, which he would finish up. This was very good training for an illustrator, but whenever I'd submit some work of my own, the publishers would reject it, and once when Ikawa went on a short trip and I had to substitute for a few days, the readers detected it at once and responded with a flood of threats to cancel their subscriptions.

"Actually I learned more outside my work than in it. Ikawa had eight or ten student employees like me, and we set up a class to study art. I also joined a study-group of Japanese-style painters of which Shinsui Ito was another member.

"When I was about nineteen I began to feel I was getting nowhere with Ikawa so I pulled my old trick of secretly packing and running away. It wasn't a very practical move, because I had only two sen in my pocket, and I ended up going back and apologizing. A little later I told Ikawa I felt I had to leave, and he got me a place in the household of a friend only a few doors away, the Kabuki actor Shucho Bando. Kabuki actors are supposed to be accomplished at poetry and painting—usually some motif associated with their name—and their fans expect mementos along those lines. Shucho wasn't very good at painting and I was supposed to do it for him, but although Ikawa painted me a sample of Shucho's motif, I wasn't very good at it either. Fortunately, Shucho's painting began to improve, but I stayed on to answer correspondence, go with him on hunting trips, and give lessons to his wife, who suddenly got very interested in art. I also became stage-struck, but nothing came of that.

"After a couple of years with Shucho I struck out on my own. I got a job at another textile dyeing shop with the understanding that after each twenty days of work I could have ten days free to study art. I seldom got my free time, and I grew bored with

58. *Flowers, Birds (1953)*   SHIGERU HATSUYAMA

making designs for dyeing, so I left after two years. However, it was at that shop that I had my first contact with woodprints: one of the old employees made prints in his spare time, and though I never made any myself, I used to watch him for hours.

"All during these years with Shucho and the textile shop I'd been submitting my drawings to periodicals regularly, and just as regularly been turned down. However, after I quit at the shop I landed a job as illustrator for a children's magazine. The salary wasn't enough to feed the family—my mother and young brother and me—and there were some rough times, but I got my start then and I've been doing children's illustrations ever since.

"I started prints at about the same time. A publisher who lived in our neighborhood, Ryoji Kumata, was enthusiastic about creative *hanga* and as a hobby put out a magazine of creative prints called *Han Geijutsu* (Print Art), often doing the printing himself from artists' blocks. At his urging I made my first prints. The magazine was never a commercial success, but it did a great deal to encourage modern prints."

In this way Hatsuyama started making prints, self-taught except for watching the old man at the textile shop. For years prints were only a hobby with him, but during World War II he found himself frozen out of illustration because he was unable to meet government specifications for patriotic content. Then he turned to prints to make a living, made a subscription series, and in 1944 held a one-man show. He and Takei were invited to join the *Hanga* Association shortly after the war ended, breaking a precedent of sorts because neither had ever submitted a print to the association shows.

"I was too poor a salesman to earn a living making prints," he says, "so I reverted to illustration and book design after the war was over." As an example of his salesmanship he cites an incident of three or four years ago, when in a rare diversion of energy he printed a number of copies of some of his prints. A dealer got wind of it and came to buy. The situation so unnerved Hatsuyama that when asked to set a price he could only fall back on his wartime price of thirty yen, this at a time when inflation had raised the prices of other artists to from three thousand to ten thousand yen. "I was quite relieved when he took all I had," he admits, "but I got hell later from Onchi."

Hatsuyama recently moved his family into a new home designed by one of Japan's rising young architects, a modern adaptation of traditional architecture. "I don't look like I belong here," he comments. "People always assume I must be the handyman." He likes to hunt, a carry-over from his days with Shucho. "Mostly I go after birds," he says; "I hate to kill rabbits, because they look like mice and so do I." The resemblance is not as pronounced as he pretends, and lies chiefly in his being small and mild-appearing. He is balding in front, and the hair that remains is wispy and usually rumpled. Horn-rimmed glasses have a tendency to slip down his nose.

"People consider my prints poor, but my pigments excellent," he says cheerfully, and while the first half of his remark is colored by modesty, it is true that, perhaps from a respect born in the dyeing shops, he pays particular attention to his pigments, some of which are very special. One color which is almost a hallmark of his prints is the blue called *ai,* a vegetable pigment made from the plant of the same name. It is one of Japan's traditional pigments, but hard to get in fine quality. Hatsuyama has a supply from the day when he was doing Japanese-style painting. The color was too dull for brush painting, but has great beauty in prints.

He applies the pigment to his blocks with a soft, thick painter's brush rather than the usual stiff brush, and uses a variable, often very light, pressure when printing. Many of his prints are made from a single, progressively carved block, additional cutting being done before each new printing stage. This means that the first printing is also the last, for the block as it ends up can be used to print only the final stage. "The block is the most beautiful thing in the whole process," he says. "After it the print is often a disappointment."

Most of Hatsuyama's prints fall into a realm of elfin fantasy created in delicate line and color. They are light and gay, with none of the psychological overtones of surrealism. Only once has

100

his fantasy been barbed; in the period of shortages just after the war ended, all the unavailable things he craved were conjured up in a print called *Studio of Want*. He particularly likes to interpret humans in terms of plants and animals and vice versa, as in *Flowers, Birds* (print 58). Other especially successful prints are *The White Horse* (print 63), *Japanese Lanterns* (print 64), *The Crying Tree,* and a series called *Children's Games.* He himself attributes the strain of fantasy in his prints to his work as an illustrator for children. "It takes an element of fantasy to hold a child's attention," he says.

A small gallery in downtown Tokyo which specializes in creative *hanga* has noted that, while most of its sales are to foreigners, the Japanese buy a good many of Hatsuyama's prints. "I think they're my fans," he says, "people who as children loved my illustrations, and buy my prints out of loyalty. They may be moved by nostalgia, too, nostalgia for the happy days of their childhood, when a touch of fantasy was all that was needed to create a bright new world where there was always a happy ending."

59. *Arrival of a Portuguese Ship* (1952)

SUMIO KAWAKAMI

60. *Nambanesque Behavior* (1955)

61. *Devils* (1952)

62. *Landscape* (1952)

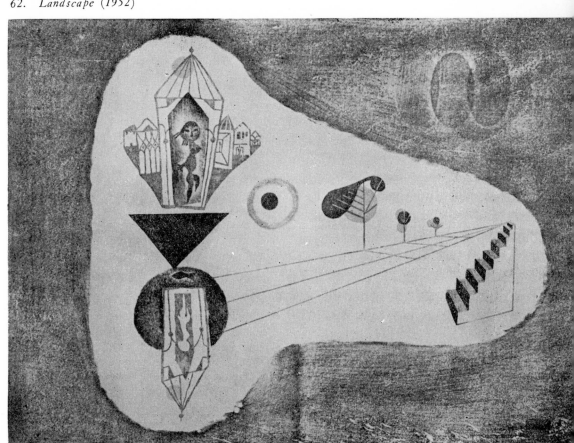

63. *The White Horse* (1948

SHIGERU HATSUYAMA

64. *Japanese Lanterns* (1952)

II
OUTSIDE OF TOKYO

Tokushi Katsuhira
Susumu Yamaguchi
Hide Kawanishi
Tomikichiro Tokuriki

QUIET, ARISTOCRATIC OLD KYOTO IS TRADITIONALLY THE CULTURAL AND artistic capital of Japan. A notable exception concerns *ukiyoe,* dazzling offshoot of the syncopated whirl in the brash young city called Edo then and Tokyo now. *Ukiyoe* may not have been Edo-born but it was certainly Edo-bred.

Though prints have always been a Tokyo art, today, in the field of creative *hanga* where publishers and a pool of artisans are no longer important, an artist can work anywhere he chooses. The men whose stories follow are representative of many other noteworthy artists who practice their art far from Tokyo and seem to thrive on it.

Not only do these four men live outside Tokyo, but their environment has put a definite stamp on their artistic personalities. In illustrating the peasant customs of his area, Tokushi Katsuhira has utilized a style which emphasizes the rustic quality of his art. Susumu Yamaguchi has concentrated on portraying the mountains among which he was born and now lives; they have furnished him

105

not only a source of subject matter but have directly affected his method of depicting their stern peaks. Hide Kawanishi's bold style is obviously influenced by the great port city of Kobe, while Tomikichiro Tokuriki's urbanity just as surely reflects Kyoto. These men are not local artists in the narrow sense, but each is very definitely marked by his locale and the influence is graphically expressed in his art.

TOKUSHI
KATSUHIRA

Tokushi Katsuhira (born 1904) is a native of Akita in the northwest part of the main island of Honshu, and his prints are exclusively devoted to the peasant life and customs of that region. Katsuhira, however, was born not on a farm but in town, to a family who did plastering in the warm weather and made paper in the cold, and of course he learned to help with both occupations.

"When I was young," he says, "my job in paper-making was to spread the newly made wet paper on the drying boards and carry them out into the sun. It kept me busy enough on sunny days, but when we were plagued by wind or rain or snow it was much worse: I was always dashing out with the boards to take advantage of a little good weather or rushing in with them when it turned bad. Somehow it seemed to me I never had a chance to play.

"We made two kinds of paper: the thin, translucent *shoji* paper for Japanese doors and a heavier paper especially for account books. Both were made from *kozo,* and it's not easy work. Steaming the branches and stripping the bark, scraping off the black outer skin, boiling and bleaching the fiber, beating it until it becomes smooth and soft, making the stock, and finally the delicate job of dipping the mold and manipulating it so as to get a strong, even sheet—none

106

of it is easy. My father, who is still living at eighty-two, was the third generation of paper-makers, but they say that my mother was even more skilful. She died when I was twelve, and it was mostly because I was lonely that I started to paint water colors in my childhood."

Katsuhira graduated from elementary school at fifteen, and as the eldest son he then set to work in earnest to learn the family trades. By this time cheap factory-made paper was beginning to cut deep into the local market, and the family began to concentrate on what had been their secondary craft, plastering of the kind used to make the hard, fire-resistant walls of warehouses. From his father Katsuhira learned how to apply the relief-work designs always used on such walls.

"I wasn't happy about either of the trades that I seemed destined for," he says, "and I turned more and more to water colors for solace. About this time I discovered the beauty of black and white prints through illustrations, and I started to make some myself for the local newspaper.

"During these years my father sent me to the cities to study cement-wall plastering, first for about six months to Tokyo and three years later to Osaka for another six months. In those cities my eyes were for the first time opened to art. I spent all the time I could spare visiting shrines and temples to look at the wood sculpture, and I'll never forget the thrill when I discovered *ukiyoe*. Kiyochika was the first artist I found and I still feel very close to him. I liked his Western approach, and the touch of sadness with which he recorded a dying period. I also admired Hiroshige, or perhaps it was his artisan-printer, for the beauty of his color is what excited me most.

"I never had a teacher in prints and I never went to art school. I've never even seen an artisan at work. Practically everything I learned I had to dig out for myself. The closest thing to instruction was talking with the editor and reporters of the newspaper. Some of them were *ukiyoe* lovers and they told me what they knew about woodblock technique and the world of art in general. When I was twenty-two I discovered on my own how to combine colors and make multicolor prints, and a couple of years later, in 1928, the *Hanga* Association accepted my prints for exhibition.

"The first professional artist I ever met was Goro Kimura, a wood sculptor who specialized in local genre. He came to Akita in 1928, and I studied with him for about a month. I had never thought I could make a living from prints, but the little figures he taught me to make sold well as gifts and as examples of handicraft. With these and prints I saw a chance to break away from the family trades, and I did."

For the next ten or twelve years Katsuhira made both prints and his little wood sculptures, but about 1940 he gave up the figures to concentrate on prints. "It was during this period," he says, "that my father made some thick, strong paper for me, especially suited for *hanga.* I use this paper for my finest prints and still have some of it left. Prints made on this paper are marked with a seal reading 'Paper made by father, Tamekichi.' "

Katsuhira's prints seem obviously influenced by his sculpture, and the figures in his prints look like the little wooden figures transplanted to appropriately simple fields and farmyards. He has consciously maintained a style to suit his rustic subjects. He considers that his finest prints are a series of four called *Rice-Making,* and subtitled *Spring, Summer, Autumn,* and *Winter;* but *Hearth* (print 66) and *Seller of Bonden* (print 67) are equally representative.

In both prints and sculpture he has never drawn on any subject matter other than local peasant customs. "It was when I first began to think about *ukiyoe,*" he says, "that I realized that the process which caused the death of that art was the same one that was killing our family trade of paper-making, and that all over the country handicrafts were giving way to mechanization. I thought a lot about culture and tradition, and I made it my aim to record for posterity the old customs which are disappearing with the passage of time. I have come to realize that this is the only way I can leave behind me work that can be appreciated by future generations."

Susumu Yamaguchi (born 1897) lives about one hundred and thirty miles west of Tokyo in the beautiful upper valley of the Tenryu River, between the central and southern ranges of the Japan Alps. His present home is only a stone's throw from the farmhouse where he was born and grew up and where, one day when he was twenty-four years old, he approached his father and told him he wanted to leave home for Tokyo.

His father, as fathers will, asked why, and when Yamaguchi replied with youthful assurance that he intended to become either a very rich man or a very great one, although he hadn't exactly decided which, the old man's answer was a firm negative. "No good," he said. "Before you can go to Tokyo you've got to have a definite plan."

"Faced suddenly with the choice of a career," says Yamaguchi, "I said the first thing that popped into my head. 'I want to be an artist,' I told him, and to that my father gave his consent. Having made a promise to him, I wanted to keep it, and I suppose that's why I'm an artist today."

Yamaguchi's decision was not quite as offhand as he makes it sound. Without training or guidance, he had been exploring art for a long time. He made his first print while he was still in grammar school. "I was intrigued by some illustrations in the newspaper," he says, "and someone told me they were made by carving on wood. I found a *baren* without difficulty, because there was a paper manufacturer in our village who printed the lines on letter paper using a wood block and *baren,* but I couldn't find any carving tools. I ended up taking the rib from an old umbrella and sharpening it to a point." Surprisingly, this first print was a color print, made without a *kento,* because he didn't know what a *kento* was, but with proper registry achieved by the simple expedient of using paper the same size as his blocks.

Later, while he was working at the local post office, he spent most of his spare time doing water colors and filling sketchbooks with decorative designs for chinaware. "I bought unpainted dishes and experimented with decorating them," he says, "wondering if I could develop items which would be saleable in Tokyo."

He had gone to work in the post office when he was seventeen. After a year or so of general clerical work he was sent for a year to the city of Nagano to learn telegraphy in the government communications school there, and then he came back to the village post office for five years as a telegrapher. "But work in the post office was stultifying, I was ambitious, and Tokyo beckoned," says Yamaguchi, "so I took the plunge."

In Tokyo he saw his first oil paintings, and because of them he felt that the sketching and designing he had done previously were worthless. He had much to learn, he decided, and he promptly enrolled in a private art school under Seiki Kuroda, who was the towering figure in the field of Western-style art in Japan, known specifically for having introduced impressionism.

A student in the daytime, Yamaguchi had to earn his living by night work. With his experience, he first landed a job in a post office, but later he found easier work as a night watchman in a government tobacco warehouse. Finally he spent three years in what he calls social welfare work, an effort typical of young men at that time. Fortified with the equivalent of about three hundred dollars collected from a few patrons, he started a sort of hostel for day laborers, with the idea of providing a decent place to live and a clearing house for jobs. "Most of these men were from the country," Yamaguchi says, "and I knew what it was for a country boy to hit Tokyo, alone and jobless, and try to make his way. I leased a huge house in the Hongo district, with room for about seventy men, and even got professors from the nearby universities to come in and give lectures. I kept it going for about three years, but I finally got discouraged and gave up. No matter what I did for them, the men drank up their money as fast as they made it, they wouldn't pay even the very modest rent I needed to keep the house going, and when they were broke they tried to force me to give them money. Once a bunch of them even drew a knife on me."

In the meantime he kept up his studies with Kuroda. "In order to show my father that I was making some progress," he says, "I tried to get my work in as many exhibitions as possible, just so I could send home the catalogs.

"My first success was in a caricature contest. I submitted seven cartoons, all of which were accepted, exhibited, and bought by one of the Wanamakers from America. I made my first print, other than my schoolboy efforts, when I saw a poster advertising an early *Hanga* Association show, and I ran into the same problem I had as a boy—trying to find tools. I finally had a blacksmith make some for me. I remember that in the artists' get-together after that show the main topic of conversation was how to obtain tools.

"But in those days I was concentrating on oils, and the other things I did were simply attempts to get into exhibitions. In one year I had thirty-six pieces accepted for different shows. I tried everything—prints, water colors, drawings, Japanese paintings. I even tried *haiga,* the little paintings which are equivalent to the *haiku* in poetry; sometimes the painting bears a *haiku* poem and sometimes not, but in any case it has a *haiku* quality—a few strokes in simple colors to convey a swift impression."

After trying all these media Yamaguchi found that not only did he like prints best, but he was having most success with them. In 1934, he sent forty-nine prints with a big show which the *Hanga* Association organized for a European tour, and when forty-five of them were sold he decided to settle down to woodblocks.

In the meantime he had started working as a student counselor in the First Higher School, a preparatory school for Tokyo Imperial University (now Tokyo University). He wanted only part-time work so he could concentrate on his art, but he kept getting more and more duties until he found himself a member of the full-time staff. He stayed there twenty years but was an active artist the entire time.

The war interrupted this life. Burned out, he evacuated to the mountains the day before the fighting stopped. "And at the age of fifty," he says, "I became a farmer." Rice is the money crop on his small farm (two-thirds of an acre and much too big, he says:

III

he's planning to sell half of it), but around him there are rich yields of apples, pears, grapes, and tobacco, with profitable silkworm culture on the side. Coming back to the land after years in the city, Yamaguchi introduced a scientific approach, and the local farmers, sceptical at first, now come to him for advice.

He was not so successful when he tried to raise cultural standards. Like Kanae Yamamoto before him, he found the local people were interested in art only if there was a prospect of money in it. "I decided I'd better start with the children," he says, "and to do that I had to cultivate the teachers." He went to work on the board of education, and now he holds a monthly class for the art teachers of a big surrounding area. He also teaches in the high school two days a week.

His farming and teaching have not kept him from making prints. The mountains have always been dominant in his work, even while he lived in Tokyo, and a print like *Tokyo Night* is an exception with him. He has become especially known for his prints of Taisho-ike (one of which is shown as print 68), a lake formed in 1915 when the volcano Yake-dake erupted and dammed the river at Kamikochi. Charred trees still stand in the quiet water beneath the scarred and smoldering peak which caused the flood, a haunting scene which Yamaguchi has successfully captured. Other outstanding prints are *Mt. Hodaka at Daybreak* (print 69), *Towards Evening,* and *Scaling the Heights.* "The mountains are deep in me," he says. "They have a sublime mystery—silent and profound."

Those who are not acquainted with Japan are usually surprised at the great regional differences among the people, largely the result of the mountain ranges which divide the country. The phrase "a Shinshu man" conjures up in the Japanese mind a type that is stubborn and assertive, that relishes argument and the pull and tug at theory, that scorns pretense and is expert at deflating it with mordant wit. Many of these regional traits apply to Yamaguchi, and indirectly to his art.

Living with the mountains all year around, he knows them too well to wish to sentimentalize them. He has eliminated everything picturesque, and the starkness of his prints conveys a sense of chill

112

greater than that of any snow scene. He has restricted the print *Mt. Hodaka at Daybreak* (print 69) to such uncompromising elements as peaks and clouds, yet the tensions set up by the composition are strong enough to dispel any possibility of monotony. It takes an accomplished artist to work with such limited subject matter and still consistently achieve results that are both creative and expressive.

The same mystical, profound quality that he associates with the mountains he finds in the woodblock prints of Gauguin. Queried as to other influences, he laughs and cites Hokusai. "When the 1934 show was exhibited in Germany," he says, "twenty-six German newspapers published reviews, and Onchi translated them for us. They were full of comments about influence: so-and-so was influenced by French impressionism, somebody else was influenced by Chinese landscapes. I was the only one for whom they named a Japanese heredity. 'Yamaguchi,' they said, 'is squarely in the tradition of Hokusai.' I'd never paid any attention to Hokusai before, but after that I thought maybe I'd better, and as a matter of fact I do like him. I like the solidity of his forms, his sense of volume, and his feeling for space."

Yamaguchi has a lively imagination in the use of carving tools, and a distinctive approach to printing. "With a creative *hanga* artist," he says, "technique is a personal and individual thing. I like to do research in technique, to develop new ideas, whatever interests me and suits my subject matter." In carving, for example, he may scrape his block with a wide rough blade, dig at it in short quick jabs, or twist his chisel back and forth to walk it across the block, creating a zigzag line; sometimes he wets his block so that the wood tears to give a jagged edge instead of a smooth one. With this rough attack it is obvious that he must usually work with solid wood rather than plywood, though much of his cutting is shallow.

His carving is so unique that much depends on his personal printing. Yamaguchi is noted among fellow artists for the amount of water he uses. Not only does he thoroughly moisten his paper (thick, specially ordered *torinoko*), but he uses an extraordinary amount of water in his pigment. Often he prints several times from the same block, gradually thickening his pigment, but in a recent shallow-cut, single-block *sumi* print he achieved variation in tone by rubbing lightly with his *baren* for several minutes: the rubbing gathered the *sumi* to the points where the block was highest, so that those portions printed darker, giving shading and form.

It is obvious that Yamaguchi the man, tall, lanky, and ruddy-faced, is very much at home among the mountains where he was born, but Yamaguchi the artist feels very much out of things since he left Tokyo. "I feel cut off," he says, "and I'm happiest when artist friends like Azechi come to visit. We talk art for hours on end. Sometimes I've felt as though I were up against a stone wall in my work, but at least there's time to think up here, and I've come to the conclusion that color photography has about taken the place of academic painting—science can do it better. Azechi used to come up here when he was battling the same problem, and I think his needling helped me to face it. 'You're letting yourself become old-fashioned,' he'd tell me, 'your art belongs to the old school. Something must be done.' Well, I have done something: I'm breaking out of the old restrictions, and I think people may be surprised at the prints I show next year." Indeed they may be, for in his recent work this previously predictable artist of mountains is exploring the realms of bold simplification and pure abstraction. The break is sharp, but he has not lost himself in the process: the new prints are still very much his own and give strong basis for belief that his transition will be a successful one.

HIDE KAWANISHI

Unlike Yamaguchi, a reluctant exile from the capital, Hide Kawanishi (born 1894) is deeply rooted in his home city, the great port of Kobe. Tall, slender, with a sharply molded face and aristocratically thin nose and lips, he is pleasantly proud of being the tenth generation to live on the same plot of land in the center of the city, proud of his hereditary name of Zen'emon VII, proud of his well-to-do merchant ancestors. The latter were traders who specialized in the manufacture of saké, *mirin* (a sweet saké used for flavoring),

114

65. *Snow at the Lakeside (1942)*   HIDE KAWANISHI

and *shochu* (a cheaper and more powerful concoction distilled from saké dregs or, more often today, sweet potatoes). These products were transported to Tokyo in the family's own fleet of ships, whose captains took the money realized there and sailed to the northern island of Hokkaido, where they loaded up with special varieties of fish and seaweed for sale back in Kobe, thus completing a profitable round trip.

There is one scanty parallel with Yamaguchi, however: Kawanishi is a postmaster. "When I was born, in this same house," he says, "my grandfather was operating a neighborhood post office in the front of the house, as I do now. In those days men operated such post offices only as a service to their community. They were specially chosen persons of character and substance—they had to be, because they received no compensation for their services and had to pay the help out of their own pockets. My father let the office lapse, but I revived it. After the war, however, post offices like this were incorporated into the regular system, and my help and I became salaried government employees.

"With its long merchant background," Kawanishi goes on, "it isn't surprising that my family was very much opposed to my becoming an artist. On the other hand, I've always wanted nothing else. Even in kindergarten, I can remember that the teacher gave me the largest sheet of paper to draw on, indicating that I was the best in the class.

"There were art classes in my grammar school, but in the commercial high school I attended there was nothing like that. Father called my drawing a waste of time, but he never refused to buy me art materials when I asked for them, and I kept on sketching and painting in water colors. I saw my first oil painting at seventeen when the government show came on tour to Kyoto. I immediately wanted to try for myself, and since there were no teachers in Kobe,

115

I enrolled in a correspondence course from Tokyo. You couldn't even buy oil paints in Kobe, and I had to order my paints from Tokyo too. Often I'd run out of paint in the middle of a picture.

"I first got excited about woodcuts when I saw Kanae Yamamoto's print *A Small Bay in Brittany* in the window of an art shop in Osaka. I'd seen *ukiyoe,* of course, but they didn't interest me. Yamamoto's print did, and I started to make a few prints along with my oils."

His father's objections continued, and finally Kawanishi promised that he would stop painting when he graduated from high school. To mark the finish he decided to hold a one-man show, and he assembled about fifty pieces, mostly oils, with some water colors, pastels, and pen drawings. But the show which was supposed to end a brief career in art proved to be more of a beginning. It made him new friends who encouraged him to continue, and scuttling his unhappy father's plans to send him to higher school, he resolved to be an artist.

He first exhibited prints with the *Hanga* Association in 1923, having learned about the association from the shows they held in Osaka. The more he worked in prints, the better he liked them, and he gradually abandoned oils. Furthermore, the circus was his favorite subject in those days, and he felt that prints were better suited to that motif than oils.

"I've never liked Japanese circuses," he says, "but fortunately, since Kobe is a great port, I was able to see foreign circuses. When the Hagenbeck Circus came from Germany, it took them four or five days to unload and set up, and I stayed with them the whole time. I desperately wanted one of their posters and I spoke my first English when I went to Mr. Hagenbeck to ask for one. He gave me a complete set, and later he wrote a foreword to a book of my circus prints.

"All my life I've liked foreign things," he goes on. "My house is filled with them, and from haunting antique shops, the very first foreign word I ever learned was 'curio.' When I was a boy I used to go to a nearby bar for sailors and watch them having a good time. I've always liked the free and easy atmosphere of a port."

As might be expected, Kawanishi likes *Nagasaki-e* (Nagasaki pictures, a type of *namban* print), finding most of his interests reflected in those old prints showing Japan's first foreign traders and their sailing ships in the port of Nagasaki. "I think," he says, "that had I lived in those days, I would have made prints like *Nagasaki-e*. They have the same exotic atmosphere I try to recreate. I believe that Sumio Kawakami and I share the same approach: we like to look at Japanese subjects through Western eyes, or Western subjects through Japanese eyes.

"When I say I like *Nagasaki-e,* however, I mean I like their atmosphere and subject matter, not their technique. In both *Nagasaki-e* and *ukiyoe* the method is black outlines filled in with color. I've tried the same thing, but I find that prints minus the outlines have more vitality. There's a feeling of incompleteness, but there is a certain beauty in incompleteness, an ever-developing imagery. The problem is to do away with the outline and yet somehow compensate for it. I don't feel I've solved the problem, but I'm still working at it.

"At any rate, where the old prints used black for explanation, tc define contours, I use it as just another color area. It's strong color, of course, but I like strong colors." This is evident, for Kawanishi has the most vivid palette among today's woodblock artists. He never mixes his colors, using them in the original hue and in bold masses.

His colors are so bright and his patterns so strong that one wonders how he avoids being gaudy, but in fact both color and pattern are under firm control, intelligently exploited in order to dominate his subject matter. *Snow at the Lakeside* (print 65), *Iris Season* (print 70), *Interior with Narcissus* (print 71)—these prints might easily have fallen into the category of mere illustration, but Kawanishi rises above illustration to catch the essence of the scene.

One of the works he is happiest about is his prewar series of *One Hundred Views of Kobe.* So many of the landmarks he pictured were destroyed in the war that the prints have become very valuable, and the city has awarded him a cultural prize. While he hadn't intended those prints as a memorial, he did make one print with just such an idea in mind: during the war he made a print of all the curios he most prizes, so that if his house were destroyed he would still have a record of them; fortunately, the house escaped damage. To date he has made almost a thousand prints. Many of them are small but among his larger works, in addition to those illustrated, *Motomachi in Early Summer, Orchestra, Antique Shop,* and *Porthole* deserve special notice. His son Sukesaburo is now making prints in much the same style as his father.

Kawanishi carves primarily with the curved chisel, the tool introduced by Yamamoto. However, where Yamamoto and other pioneers used it to achieve tone over a flat area, Kawanishi uses it to carve his contours, preferring the soft edge he gets that way to the harder edge made by a straight chisel. He uses solid blocks of *katsura* or *ho,* and prints on thick *hodomura* paper, thoroughly moistened so that the colors seep through to the back.

As influences, he cites Lautrec and van Gogh, remarking on Lautrec's love of the circus. He adds that some of Matisse and Leger have furnished "food," though he doesn't consider them a direct influence. In prints he names Yamamoto, Onchi, and, like so many others, Gauguin. "Today the exotic is no longer very strange," he says, "but when I was young it was new. It kindled my senses and caught my imagination—permanently, I guess, because I still feel the same excitement." His strong, vivid prints reveal that excitement and continue to project it.

TOMIKICHIRO TOKURIKI

Friendly, urbane Tomikichiro Tokuriki (born 1902) is a leader among the print artists of Kyoto. He says: "Fate made me an artist, but I made myself a *hanga* artist." As eldest son he continues an unbroken line of artists which can be traced back at least as far as the Keicho era (1596–1615). He has a painting by the first known Tokuriki artist, and he unrolls the scroll to show the portrait of an insouciant young lady with diverting eyes. "She was his daughter," says Tokuriki, and looking across the generations to his so-many-times-great-aunt, one knows that the past is very near in Kyoto.

That earliest Tokuriki was a pupil of Sansetsu Kano, a master of the Kyoto line of Kano artists, and all the Tokurikis up to the present have been painters of the Kano school—a bit of information that may tell less about their styles of painting than their family loyalties. "In this long line," says Tokuriki, "I am the first *hanga* artist," though he adds that his father did a few small prints like greeting cards, carved and printed by artisans. "I still have those blocks here in the house," he says with a smile. "In Kyoto we never throw anything away."

Rather than these casual efforts by his father, he thinks that his interest in prints stems from the work of his maternal grandfather, an artist and teacher. "During his lifetime he made seventy-two flower prints," says Tokuriki. "When I was a child I loved to look at them, and they were my introduction to *hanga*."

As one would expect, Tokuriki received impressive training in Japanese painting: the two-year preparatory and four-year art courses of the Kyoto school of arts and crafts, and then the three-year course at the Kyoto art college, from which he graduated in 1923. It was while he was at the school of arts and crafts that he began to make *sosaku hanga*. "The creative-print movement was beginning to get underway in Tokyo," he says. "The atmosphere was warming up, and amateurs were starting to try their hand."

His interest spurted when a number of Tokyo publishers and artisans moved to Kyoto after Tokyo's earthquake of 1923. "In a sense," says Tokuriki, "the art was coming home, for woodcuts were first made here and in Nara when they were introduced from China in the eighth century as part of our Buddhist heritage. Of course, a thousand years went by before the dazzling technique of *ukiyoe* evolved, and that development took place in Edo. Here in Kyoto the art survived only in two stagnant lines: one continued to print the Buddhist scriptures for the temples as they had for centuries, and another did rather crude commercial work like wrapping papers.

"It's true that there had been reproductive prints made in Kyoto before 1923, but these men from Tokyo were a shot in the arm for woodcuts here. I became seriously interested and decided to study technique. I found a fine old printer in the direct line of the *ukiyoe* tradition—as a young man he had printed for Hiroshige III—and asked him to come to my studio and teach me. I learned carving from another artisan, going to his place to work out my problems."

This artisan training, which shows in Tokuriki's professional-looking blocks, has also made him particular about his pigments. Being close to Nara, where much of Japan's *sumi* is made, Tokuriki is able to buy the shavings which result when the blocks of ink are trimmed after being taken from the mold, an ingenious way of getting fine *sumi* very cheaply. His paper is *hosho* from Echizen, sized and moistened, says Tokuriki, "just as I was taught."

"It was only a little after I'd seriously turned to prints that Hiratsuka came to Kyoto to teach a short course, spreading the doctrine of creative prints. Since I had some training I assisted him and in that way received an introduction to the Tokyo artists. I joined the *Hanga* Association and actively participated in a magazine called *Han* put out by a group close to Hiratsuka, men like Masao Maeda, Kihachiro Shimozawa, Hide Kawanishi, and Shiko Munakata. It was a good magazine, but like all the rest, short-lived. I lost touch with the association during the war, and I don't know whether they still consider me a member or not."

Tokuriki's two younger brothers have also made careers in art. One works in lacquer, teaching that technique at the Kyoto art university, which is the successor to the Kyoto art college and has absorbed Tokuriki's other alma mater, the school of arts and crafts. The other brother is a potter, having studied with the famous Kenkichi Tomimoto.

For a sure source of income Tokuriki sells tea in the shop which fronts his two-hundred-year-old house. A friendly priest told him that the saint Daruma (Dharma in India) brings particular good luck to enterprises involving tea, and so the shop is named Daruma-do

120

and its sign bears the round-bottomed likeness which is a favorite symbol in Japan—no matter how you push it around it always rolls upright again. When Tokuriki serves tea he accompanies it with little sweet cakes made in the image of Daruma from a mold designed by his potter brother.

Just as he keeps his tea business apart from his art, so he has two lines as an artist. For bread and butter, or the Japanese equivalents, he does artisan prints; for his own satisfaction he makes creative prints. For his artisan prints he has developed a colorful style with obvious sales appeal, and his reputation as a print artist in Japan rests largely on the several popular series of landscapes which have been a source of tidy profit to various Kyoto publishers.

On the other hand, he publishes his creative prints himself. "I keep the two kinds of work separate," he says. "I'd rather do nothing but creative prints, but after all, I sell maybe ten of them against two hundred for a publisher-artisan print." Looking to a brighter day, Tokuriki uses his artisan prints to subsidize his creative prints, and continues the fight to revitalize *hanga* in Kyoto.

It may seem strange to talk about Kyoto artists as though they were a separate movement, but in many respects Kyoto and Tokyo are farther apart than the three hundred and twenty miles between them. Kyoto sees itself as the repository of culture and tradition and bestows a dowager's disdain on upstart, new-rich Tokyo. This feeling cuts deep in many ways, and while it would be naïve to suggest that it explains the difference in creative prints today, it does help to account for a certain aloofness on the part of the Kyoto artists.

In discussing Kyoto prints, Dr. Fujikake has said that they suggest painting rather than woodblock, and Tokuriki agrees with him. "I know that we adhere very closely to the brush stroke," he says. "Perhaps Kyoto print artists are too accomplished technically. We were never gripped by the same rebellion against *ukiyoe* technique that motivated the Tokyo artists, and while not all of the men here sought out artisans for training as I did, they have all worked to acquire the same discipline, and they're proud of it; they like to point this up by saying: 'Tokyo artists can't get a hundred copies from their blocks.'" (It would be interesting to hear the Tokyo artist's retort to this.)

If one asks why the Kyoto artists cling to an artisan approach, Tokuriki answers that the *hanga* artists of Tokyo developed from Western-style painters trained in oil, while the Kyoto artists are men whose background is Japanese painting in *sumi* and water color. There is little friendship between oil and the chisel, but Japanese painting gets on very well with the carving tools. Thus the artist who turns to woodblock from oil is in revolt and seeking a new mode of expression, but the artist who moves to prints from Japanese painting makes a smooth transition to a medium compatible with the style he was trained to; if he wants to break away from mere reproduction of that line and stroke, he has to fight to do it.

Tokuriki's artisan prints reveal how closely the woodblock can be made to conform to the water color, but the best of his creative prints, like *Woman Combing Her Hair* (print 72) and *Sanjo Bridge* (print 73), show a resolute effort to design with the knife. "I want to break away from the brush," says Tokuriki. "That's the reason I've been making black and white prints like the *Ten Oxherding Pictures*." This modern interpretation of an old Zen parable shows an oxherder who has carelessly lost his ox—the Essential Truth—and his struggles to find and recapture the beast. Though the parallel is far from exact, Tokuriki has experienced a somewhat similar struggle as he has worked to free himself from training and tradition and to forge a style rooted in his medium. Happily, one can stretch the parallel a little further, for it seems certain that, like the oxherder, Tokuriki will succeed.

66. *Hearth (1939)*

TOKUSHI
KATSUHIRA

67. *Seller of*
Bonden (1935)

68. *Taisho-ike (1952)*

SUSUMU YAMAGUCHI

69. *Mt. Hodaka at Daybreak (1955*

70. *Iris Season (1955)*

HIDE
KAWANISHI

71. *Interior with Narcissus (1947)*

72. *Woman Combing Her Hair (1947)*

TOMIKICHIRO
TOKURIKI

73. *Sanjo Bridge (1954)*

12

HIRATSUKA'S CIRCLE:
THE YOYOGI GROUP

KIHACHIRO SHIMOZAWA
MASAO MAEDA
OKIIE HASHIMOTO
UMETARO AZECHI

NO MAN HAS WORKED LONGER, HARDER, AND MORE CONSISTENTLY AT HIS art than Un'ichi Hiratsuka. Consistency stamps him: in the forty years he has been producing prints his massive output has been amazingly stable. A slow development toward simplication, an occasional accent like his change to the jagged line, mark the steady course of this quiet, most unvolatile artist.

Apart from his own work, Hiratsuka is a dedicated teacher. "I want to pass on what I learned from Igami," he says, "so that younger men will have some knowledge of the traditional way. But I never insist that they follow that way: I try to teach them the possibilities of each tool, and then encourage them to develop their own ideas." He adds: "I've found that to teach others is to teach oneself. I learn something from every student, no matter how young and naïve."

Through the years he has taught many artists. Masaji Yoshida, Fumio Kitaoka, and Thoru Mabuchi took his course at Ueno. Tomoo Inagaki, Kihei Sasajima, Tomikichiro Tokuriki, and Shiko Munakata studied with him less formally. With all of these men his influence was relatively fleeting, a brief exposure to traditional technique. In contrast, the four men discussed in this chapter are linked with him by a real affinity. They illustrate one of the two main trends today, the revitalization of the Japanese tradition in representational art, just as Onchi and his followers illustrate the other line, the Western path toward symbolism reduced to final abstraction. Hiratsuka and these men are sublimating Western art to a deeply Japanese expression, and they have a sense of immediacy to their native scene which makes them seem much more Japanese than most of the other artists in this book.

Except for Okiie Hashimoto, they began their association in the 1920's, at a time when Hiratsuka was living in the Yoyogi section of Tokyo and the others were renting rooms in the same neighborhood. It is interesting that, on the surface at least, these men appear to have drifted into prints and drifted to Hiratsuka, but once met they have remained close. Hiratsuka was not many years older, but those few years were important ones: he was an established artist and they were still struggling. They needed help and encouragement, and he gave it to them, as the story of each reveals.

KIHACHIRO SHIMOZAWA

Says Kihachiro Shimozawa (born 1901): "I was the first of the Yoyogi group to get to know Hiratsuka. I've always tried to keep up the association. I owe more to him than to anyone else."

With no formal training in art, Shimozawa is largely self-taught. The art bug bit him when he was a boy of twelve or thirteen, at home in Honshu's northernmost prefecture, Aomori. A young artist who had just graduated from Ueno came to visit Shimozawa's brother-in-law and took the boy along on his sketching trips. Fascinated by the world that opened up before him, Shimozawa sat beside his new friend and sketched in pencil as the artist worked in oil. It was the first time Shimozawa had seen an oil painting.

The artist left, but the boy's enthusiasm did not. For the next couple of years he worked on his own, sketching in both pencil and water color, and then he decided it was time to come to Tokyo. He got himself a job as an office boy with an art magazine and set about to profit from his environment. There was no time to go to art school—his hours were long and he had only one or two days off a month—but he spent all his spare time on his sketching and on a new enthusiasm, print-making, and he buttonholed every good-natured artist who came into the offices. He met Hiratsuka that way and plied him with questions about the technique of the wood-block. After a while Hiratsuka began to pass odd jobs to the boy, such as running off a few prints from blocks that had been carved on a commission from a publisher. Another artist who appeared often, and thereby became an influence on the ambitious boy, was Hakutei Ishii, but Shimozawa seems to have had his advisers departmentalized: Ishii was shown only water colors.

In 1921 Shimozawa was drafted for two years of service in the army. When he got out he renewed his friendship with Hiratsuka and became a charter member of the Yoyogi group, along with Masao Maeda and Umetaro Azechi. There is no doubt that this association was important in making Shimozawa a print artist. "We even caught Hiratsuka's enthusiasm for early Buddhist prints," he says, "and poor as we were, we used to scour the curio shops hunting them. They were still available then, and cheap." And he goes on: "None of us had any money, but we were young and high-spirited and determined to be artists. We would meet at Hiratsuka's house and tear each other's work apart. Then each of us would pull himself together and go back to his room, resolved to produce something that would make the others admit it was good.

"I live from my prints now," he says. "No commercial art—I'm no good at it. But I must admit that for many long years after I got out of the army, while I was still learning, I lived off my brother. To get money I had to make fairly frequent trips back home. It was on one of these trips, in 1924, that I first met Munakata, also an Aomori boy. I met him when I went to have lunch with another artist. Munakata, a blacksmith's son, had walked ten miles to get there and arrived soaked with sweat and so hungry they had to cook an extra pot of rice. After lunch we climbed to a shrine on a nearby mountain. We carved our names on the shrine and vowed that the first to get a picture accepted by the government show would be the 'big brother' of our little group. I made it the next year with a tempera painting.

"I believe that Munakata became interested in prints through me," he adds. "I taught him something about woodblocks in Aomori, and once he told me that he couldn't compete with me in color, so he was going to restrict himself to black and white. After he came to Tokyo I introduced him to Hiratsuka, and he studied with Hiratsuka a bit, but they were poles apart in temperament, and their relationship was brief and superficial."

Shimozawa exhibited his first print with the *Hanga* Association in 1924, at a time when men like Hiratsuka, Onchi, and Maekawa were established, but Munakata, Saito, Sekino, Shinagawa, and their generation were yet to be heard from. From then until 1936 he exhibited both prints and paintings in tempera (a medium new in Japan when he started with it). In 1936 he quit tempera to concentrate on prints.

For the past fifteen years he has lived in the outer reaches of Tokyo, surrounded by farms. He is deeply tanned, with closely clipped grey hair, almost bald on top. Though not a small man, there is something slightly elfin about him: he moves in quick darts, and he laughs lightly and frequently, bobbing his head as he tosses out a remark or recalls an anecdote.

"My technique is the traditional one as taught me by Hiratsuka," he says, "and my whole idea is to continue the tradition of *ukiyoe,* but as a creative art form dominated by the artist rather than the artisan. It's a process of bringing *ukiyoe* under the control of the artist by his ability to do his own carving and printing, and also, I think, a process of simplification. In this I believe I'm following

130

in Hiratsuka's path." This point of view is underlined when he names two *ukiyoe* artists as strong early influences: Hiroshige and Kiyochika (the same two men, incidentally, admired by Katsuhira).

Typical of his work are mountain landscapes, large figures, and, recently, prints which have as their motif a window or a doorway. It is especially in his mountain prints that one sees his relationship to the landscapes of *ukiyoe*. A print like *Ikari-ga-Seki* (print 76) is very close to the work of artists like Hiroshige in the sense that it catches the warmth and intimacy of the Japanese countryside. This is a very different approach from that of men like Susumu Yamaguchi, Masao Maeda, and Umetaro Azechi, to whom the same mountains are a point of departure for creating an intellectual and poetic simplification.

By the Window (print 75) reveals Shimozawa's trend away from the *ukiyoe* tradition to a stronger and more personal expression. It has been said that his prints have been influenced by his hobby, the seventeen-syllable verse form called *haiku*. This is debatable, for certainly there is nothing in his prints similar to *haiga*, the fleet little paintings based directly on *haiku*, as described by Susumu Yamaguchi. If the influence exists it is to be seen in the simplification of this print, the use of a few evocative symbols to set a mood. Says Shimozawa: "People who read my poems say they're reminded of my prints, so I suppose there is a relationship. But isn't that natural? After all, they're both mine."

Masao Maeda (born 1906) has liked art ever since he can remember, and by the fifth grade he had already decided to become an artist. This was in the city of Hakodate, on the northern island of Hokkaido, where he was born and raised. In 1924 he came to Tokyo and entered a private art school to study Western oil painting, but, dissatisfied with the instruction he was getting, he quit after two years and went to study with Ryuzaburo Umehara, the noted oil painter already mentioned in connection with the art association Kokuga-kai. Maeda started to exhibit his oils in 1927.

MASAO
MAEDA

131

MASAO MAEDA

During this early period he did not work in prints, and yet, he says: "I was very conscious of them. A year or so before I left Hakodate a group of Tokyo artists came there to hold a show. Hiratsuka was among them and I met him then. When I came to Tokyo I lived near him and we were together in Kokuga-kai. I used to visit him often. I was treated like one of the family, and watching him carve from morning till night, I picked up technique and naturally started to make prints myself."

Maeda started exhibiting prints in the early 1930's. Throughout the 30's he showed both oils and prints, but since 1940 he has shown only prints. He now makes a living from his prints, selling them directly or at exhibitions.

"I think that woodprints suit the character of a Japanese," he says. "The materials are close to our life: wood, paper, even the *baren* with its bamboo cover. I think of trying etchings and lithographs but I never get around to them, and though I like Onchi's ideas of utilizing all sorts of odd materials, I just can't get away from wood."

Maeda thinks that he has been influenced by his old teacher Umehara, by Renoir, Matisse, and Braque, and it is evident that he has been exposed to sophisticated currents in both Western and Japanese painting. *Big Haul Net* (print 77) and *Black Cat* (print 78) demonstrate that in both composition and subject matter he is very close to contemporary Japanese-style painting: it may well be that his medium is the more logical one for treating these ideas. He feels that in prints the influence of Hiratsuka has permeated him thoroughly. "But I've tried to broaden myself," he says. "I've especially come to admire the cleanness and wood quality of Maekawa's prints, and I think I've learned much from Onchi's work: most important, perhaps, freedom, an unshackling which means a great deal.

"Onchi used to hold monthly group meetings and I tried very

132

hard not to miss them. They started informally. Artists were always going to see Onchi, and Sekino got the idea of meeting together regularly. It was easier on Onchi and we could share each other's criticism. We met the first Thursday of every month and called ourselves Ichimoku-kai, which was a sort of pun: it can be read either as 'First Thursday Club' or 'Best Prints Club.' Onchi was very democratic and the discussion was free and easy. Sekino, Shinagawa, Saito, Gen Yamaguchi, Kitaoka, and Azechi attended regularly, and I think those meetings were important to all of us."

Lines were important in his earlier prints; but now masses predominate, and his colors are heavy and vivid. He quite often uses one cardboard block in a print to get shadings. His work tends to still life and landscape, typical prints other than those reproduced being *Peaches, Canna,* and *Fishing Village.* He has done several prints of mountains, among them *Togakushi* and *Yake-ga-Take,* but he is no ardent mountaineer like Azechi and climbs only for the sake of getting a picture. "A true mountaineer always has to get to the top," he says, "but the finest panoramas are down in the middle heights. That's where I stop."

Okiie Hashimoto (born 1899) took the teacher's training course in the government art school at Ueno. In this three-year course he received a broad education in almost every field of art: a partial list of subjects includes oil painting, Japanese-style painting, sculpture, applied design, etching and lithography, crafts, calligraphy, and art history; and in addition, of course, there was liberal training and practice in teaching methods. "To the extent that I was allowed to," he says, "I specialized in oil painting, and all

OKIIE
HASHIMOTO

133

through my teaching carrer I have specialized in Western art— oil, water colors, and pastels." When he was graduated from Ueno in 1924 he started teaching in the public schools of Tokyo, at a middle school which is now coeducational but was then a girls' school, and he has taught at the same school ever since. It seems to have agreed with him, and with his vigorous, pleasant, straightforward personality he seems the ideal teacher. In addition to his teaching he has been serving on three different committees for the Education Ministry, with the tasks of choosing texts and materials and planning the nation's art courses. "It's kept me busy," he says, "and up to now I've been a Sunday print-maker. After more than thirty years of teaching I think I've earned retirement, and this will be my last year. From now on I'm going to devote full time to my prints. My school has been fine about it, and now they're urging me to have a one-man show. I'm looking forward to my new freedom and time to work on my prints." One guesses that the change will be less retirement than a shift in careers, and that Hashimoto will be as busy as ever.

"I started making woodblocks while I was still in art school," he says, "but only minor things like greeting cards. It wasn't until about 1932 that I became seriously interested. I heard that Hiratsuka was to give a short course and I decided to take it. Though it only lasted three days, in that time Hiratsuka introduced the whole range of technique, and that was the only formal training in woodblocks I've ever had; since then I've worked out my problems on my own. However, I did become friends with Hiratsuka—we're from the same part of the country—and I know that deepened my interest in prints." This is understandable, for the two men have much in common artistically; Hashimoto's castles, especially, reveal the same attitude that Shimozawa expressed: a continuation of the tradition of *ukiyoe,* simplified and revitalized.

"Print-making suits me," he goes on. "I've worked in both oil and Japanese water color and I keep them up, water colors for relaxation and oils to stay in practice; besides I use both to make sketches for my prints. But as a medium I much prefer prints. I feel I can get more expression from the carving tool than I ever can from the brush. The brush goes along too easily. I like the resistance that the block gives me. And don't be misled," he adds, showing the calluses which have formed on his knuckles from the pressure of the *baren,* "the whole process of making a print is hard work—it's hard but satisfying."

Speaking of artistic influences, he looks back to his student days when he admired the work of the Japanese painter Kanji Maeda, and he feels that through him he received the influence of men like Matisse, Derain, and Vlaminck. In prints he cites Hiratsuka and, like Masao Maeda, he has been attracted by the warmth of Maekawa.

"I like to sketch on the spot," he says, "and I use the line of traditional Japanese painting because I think it has something in common with the line of prints." He makes a series of sketches, culminating in a full-scale water color. On small prints he may transfer the design to the block by carbon paper, but on big prints— and some of his prints are very big, so big he makes them in sections to be pasted together—he makes a tissue based on the final sketch and pastes the tissue to his block. He plans the color blocks from the proof of the main block. "The great temptation is to lean on the sketches," he says, "but the problem is to make the blocks live, and to do that requires much more than to reproduce the sketches."

He has made several prints for a publisher, and for these he carved the blocks but an artisan did the printing. For such prints he made the main block of *sakura* and the other blocks of *katsura,* but for his own prints he usually makes the blocks of plywood faced with *shina.* His work is meticulous, and in this respect too one feels that he likes the discipline which print-making imposes.

A recent portrait of a girl illustrates some of his experiments in technique. He has combined three techniques. For the face and hair he used wood blocks. For the background and clothing he used stencils cut from the stiff waterproof paper which is used to stencil cloth; he used five stencils in all, applying oil pigment with a roller. And finally, to picture a lacy ribbon, he used a mimeograph stencil, again with oil color and a roller. He is not certain whether he will continue to use stencils, but he does plan to use oil colors with his wood blocks.

135

He has done so many prints of Japan's old castles that some people think he does nothing else. *Young Woman and Iris* (print 79) and *Nudes* demonstrate his versatility, but for most people his reputation rests on such strong, vivid, yet evocative prints as *Castle in Autumn* (print 80), *Matsumoto Castle,* and *Himeji Castle in the Snow.* "I like architectural detail and I have a special feeling for the old stone walls," he says, revealing another attitude in which he is close to Hiratsuka. "It's tragic how fast the castles are disappearing. I'd like to make a series of prints of some of the great ones at various times of the day so that people in the future will have some idea what they looked like. They're important to Japan, and important to me."

UMETARO AZECHI

The story of Umetaro Azechi (born 1902), as he tells it, makes it sound as though he became a print artist because he passed Un'ichi Hiratsuka's house while taking a walk one evening. Azechi himself feels that such random events have largely shaped his life. "I was too busy trying to earn enough to live on to plan a career," he says, but it is obvious that, through it all, he was kept going by a burning desire to be an artist.

He was born on a farm in Ehime Prefecture, on the island of Shikoku. The family was poor and could afford to send him only through elementary school, but somehow he scraped together enough money to take correspondence lessons in Western art from a school in Tokyo; he would send in drawings, water colors, and even oils; the school would send back criticism and suggestions.

At nineteen he struck out for Tokyo, got himself a job delivering newspapers, and kept up his correspondence course. About this time another student taking the same lessons got from the school the names of its seven most diligent students, a list which included himself, and then wrote to the others, among them Azechi, suggesting that they get together. They did, and it was the first time in his life that Azechi met anyone else who was trying to be an artist.

They named their little group the "Seven Stars," and they planned big things, which never materialized. Today the group's chief claim to fame is that the faculty member who offered to act as their adviser, later, after making his mark as an artist, further distinguished himself by committing one of postwar Japan's most sensational crimes, the mass murder of twelve bank employees. He accomplished this feat by announcing himself as a public health officer and giving each employee a stiff dose of "medicine"—actually potassium cyanide—after which he proceeded to rob the bank. The same man had earlier crossed the path of another of the Yoyogi group: he had been an office boy alongside Shimozawa.

Still coping with the unfriendly dogs on his newspaper route, Azechi took and passed the entrance examinations to a private art school, but when he went to enroll he found that he had to pay a year's tuition in advance. This stopped him and, discouraged, he went back home to Shikoku. Here he was called up by the army, but failure to pass the physical examination so cheered him that the he decided to take another crack at Tokyo.

He couldn't get his old job back because he'd stayed away too long, but now he had a few friends in Tokyo, and with their help he managed to get a delivery job with the Mainichi newspapers. He was on Mainichi's payroll long enough to draw one month's wages when the earthquake of 1923 razed the city. A week later he boarded an evacuation ship going back to Shikoku, with all his belongings in a briefcase.

"I had neither trade nor training," he says, "and I didn't know how I could earn a living back home. Then I found that a local movie theatre wanted a sign painter, and with the bravado of youth I announced myself as an experienced oil painter and landed the job. I stayed at it for about two years, and it was during this time that I made up my mind that, somehow, I would be an artist. So once again I headed back to Tokyo."

137

This time he found the leader of the old "Seven Stars" working in a government printing office, and with his introduction Azechi managed to get a job there. The plant had engraving equipment, and he started to experiment by scratching pictures on the soft lead plates and making impressions of them with printer's ink. "I knew nothing about engraving or etching," he says. "I was just following my natural instincts. And some things I had seen my father do came back to me. He was a skilled wood carver, who was always asked to make the masks for the festivals in our village. Once, I remember, he used a mask as a sort of block to make an ink impression on paper."

In his spare time Azechi continued to study art. While he had been working at the theatre in Shikoku he had met the sister of a prominent artist, Mango Kobayashi, and she had told him to look up her brother if he decided to study art in Tokyo. Armed with this introduction, he took some of his drawings and went to see the great man. "The first two or three attempts I was not allowed past the front door. On the final occasion Kobayashi came to the entry and, standing with his hands stuck in his belt, inspected the drawings which I spread out on the floor for him, punctuating his criticism by using his toe as a pointer. That," says Azechi, "was the last time I called on Kobayashi."

A farm boy, Azechi liked to walk, and he covered a good deal of Tokyo. One fateful evening he discovered the house of Un'ichi Hiratsuka. He didn't have the nerve to go in, but a few nights later he summoned his courage and, taking some of his lead-plate pictures, went to call.

"Hiratsuka was kind," says Azechi. "He invited me in, showed me his own work, and encouraged me about my lead-plate prints. After that I went to see him often."

Hiratsuka urged him to submit some of his pictures to the annual *Hanga* Association exhibition. To Azechi's pleased surprise they were not only accepted but were praised by Tsuruzo Ishii, and one was reproduced in the magazine *Mizue*.

The next year Hiratsuka persuaded him to submit to Kokuga-kai. This time his things were rejected, but the following year Azechi bounced back, and deciding to play both ends against the middle,

138

74. *Staring at the Snow and Ice* (1953)   UMETARO AZECHI

he violated local ethics by submitting work to two associations. He was embarrassed when both submissions were accepted and exhibited simultaneously in the same building, but to his relief no one seemed to notice—an indication, perhaps, of the insularity of Japan's art groups.

"Having had work accepted by two major groups gave me a lot of prestige at the printing plant," says Azechi, "but it didn't get me a raise in pay. Then when I was refused a bonus because I had been absent from work one or two days too many I was really miffed, and I quit. I have free-lanced ever since."

The next five or six years were hard. Often he had no money to buy food, and in desperation he would visit Hiratsuka just to get the snack that almost always appears for a visitor. But Hiratsuka was far from rich himself, and sometimes the snack never materialized.

The big event of the period came when he won a prize of a hundred yen for a woodblock print entered in a show organized by Hiratsuka. He also sold five or six copies of this print on the strength of the prize, one to an imperial prince and another to a soap tycoon. This little flurry of success decided him, he says now, to give up oils and become a print artist.

He took the whole prize to his landlord, a maker of *geta,* the Japanese wooden clogs. "My room cost me six yen a month," he says, "and I was so far behind that the whole hundred yen didn't pay my back rent, but they were overjoyed to get it. Three days later I had to borrow back twenty yen."

Mostly he kept going in those days by the occasional jobs as an artisan printer which Hiratsuka managed to pass to him. Gradually he picked up similar commissions from the other artists, especially Onchi and Maekawa, printing their work for some early series. It is to these three men that he feels he owes the most. "I'm grateful to Hiratsuka for his initial encouragement and his steady support all through the years," says Azechi. "Maybe without him I wouldn't be an artist today. As for my work, the greatest influence was Onchi, and my simplified style today owes most to him.

"Onchi was very easy to work for," he recalls. "*Sosaku hanga* printed by someone else is never perfect, but Onchi wasn't fussy and he never complained. What's more, in those days Onchi was the richest of the artists because of his success in book design, and he served the biggest lunches of any of them. I'll never forget the pleasure of those lunches.

"It was to Maekawa that I turned with my personal problems. He was more like me, simple and unsophisticated, and I leaned on him for advice about my life. My affection for Maekawa is very deep.

"Don't get the idea that I was alone in my poverty in those early days," he says. "I had a lot of friends in the same fix, and most of us in the Yoyogi group made frequent visits to the pawn shop."

Today he makes a living partly from his prints, partly from commercial design (magazine covers, match boxes, and such things), and partly from writing on the subject he has made his own in art: mountains and mountaineering.

"My work falls in four stages," he says. "First, seascapes and marines. Second, city scenes. Third, mountains, and now, figures of mountain people. I'm not really sure why I turned to the mountains. I think it was because I don't like to sketch where there are people around watching me. This led me to the mountains, and I became interested in climbing.

"Most of my mountaineering friends can't believe I'm an artist, and none of them like my prints. Their love for the mountains is very literal, and they strongly object that I change the forms of the peaks in my prints.

"My roots are in the country," he goes on, "and I like simple, rustic work. I don't like slickness or sophistication. That is why I respect Munakata's approach, and I agree with him that Japanese artists imitate too much. In my own case I think my lack of training saves me from that kind of thing—I mean I don't have the technique to be able to skip from style to style. I've never had a chance to give much thought to art movements or foreign artists until just lately. Now I'm beginning to be aware of some of the things that other men are doing."

140

That Azechi has kept his native freshness is shown by prints like *Staring at the Snow and Ice* (print 74), *Mountaineer* (print 81), *Remains of a Volcano* (print 82), and *Mountain Village*.

In making his prints, Azechi usually carves with a flat, straight-end chisel, then scrapes the edge of the line to soften and roughen it. He also roughens the surface of his flat areas so that they will catch more color. When he applies color to his blocks he brushes it on first in the usual way and then tamps more color into the block for deeper penetration. He generally prints five copies at one sitting.

Today Azechi, a long, hard pull behind him, lives with his wife and young children in a little mass-produced house on the outskirts of Tokyo, where the truck gardens begin. Met on the street with his mountaineer's cap, he looks younger than his years. At home you can see the grey in his hair, but his tanned face and arms and tough, stocky body are evidence of the time he spends in the mountains. He has achieved some success and is beginning to look about him. His story as an artist is not finished. How he develops will be interesting to watch.

75. *By the Window (1954)*

KIHACHIRO SHIMOZAWA

76. *Ikari-ga-Seki (1949)*

77. *Big Haul Net* (1941)

MASAO MAEDA

78. *Black Cat* (1940)

79. *Young Woman and Iris (1952)*

OKIIE HASHIMOTO

80. *Castle in Autumn (1954)*

81. Mountaineer (1953)

UMETARO
AZECHI

82. Remains of a
Volcano (1952)

13
THE INFLUENCE
OF ONCHI

Masaji Yoshida
Fumio Kitaoka
Gen Yamaguchi

BY NOW IT MUST BE CLEAR THAT NO INFLUENCE IN JAPANESE CREATIVE prints is as great or as pervasive as that of Koshiro Onchi. He never felt any great call as a teacher, but his work, his personality, and his character brought young artists flocking to him. His Ichimoku-kai meetings dominated the scene for ten years and were important in molding many of the artists now in their maturity; Kiyoshi Saito, Jun'ichiro Sekino, Takumi Shinagawa—these men were in different ways deeply affected by him. A few years later another, younger generation turned to him in the same way and he helped them find their bearings. Today his ideas seem more vital than ever.

His influence on the work of older artists, his contemporaries, was, naturally enough, not great, but among the younger men his effect is incalculable. Said one young artist: "I never heard him say of anything, 'That's bad.' He was always interested in new ideas. He was always looking for the good in whatever came along." And again: "Tearing down the old to make way for the new is a normal process. A favorite pastime for younger artists is to attack the work

147

of the older men. But I have never heard any young artist say he disliked Onchi, and in that he was absolutely unique."

His presence was felt in varied ways. A large number of artists felt a personal influence, powerful though not immediately obvious in their work: thus Azechi feels indebted for the simplification that makes his prints what they are today, and Maeda is grateful for a sense of "freedom, an unshackling which means a great deal." A smaller number of artists, like the men considered in this chapter, felt a much more direct influence: they shared his artistic vision and their relationship was very close.

Gen Yamaguchi, Masaji Yoshida, and Fumio Kitaoka were all affected by Onchi at critical points in their careers, Yoshida and Kitaoka in the postwar years, Yamaguchi almost a generation earlier. There are many parallels in the careers of Yoshida and Kitaoka: they are about the same age; they became friends at Ueno, where both took the course in oil painting and also studied print-making with Hiratsuka; both were caught up by the war, though in different ways; after the war, both turned from oils to prints, and as they moved towards abstract art, were deeply influenced by Onchi. The prints of these two are so much in the general stream of modern art that they could have been done anywhere in the world; in contrast, the prints of the older man, Yamaguchi, seem more Japanese and, at the same time, more closely identified with his medium.

MASAJI YOSHIDA

Masaji Yoshida (born 1917) was born in Wakayama and lived there until he finished middle school. Then he came to Tokyo, and after studying drawing from casts for a year at a private preparatory school he entered the government art academy at Ueno. It was in this period that Hiratsuka was teaching his extracurricular course in *hanga*. "I enjoyed the class," says Yoshida. "I had no idea of making prints, but I liked them and I thought it would be interesting to know more about them."

Graduating from Ueno in 1942, Yoshida was immediately drafted into the army. Within a week he was on his way to China, and

148

after a month's basic training there he was sent to the front. A year later he was back in Kyushu for six months' officers' training, and he returned to China as a warrant officer. This time he drew a commanding officer who liked art, and for the first time since Ueno he was given some free time to sketch. He was promoted to sublieutenant and then, seriously wounded in action, was hospitalized for six months, still in China.

With the armistice, his unit became prisoners of war and it was more than half a year before they were returned to Japan. Although a captive, he had freedom to roam about and sketch, and often he exchanged a drawing for a bowl of noodles. When he found he would be allowed to bring no sketches back to Japan he gave them all to the peasants.

He was repatriated in March 1946, and after a couple of weeks at home he went back to Ueno for a year of postgraduate work. "We lived like vagrants in that first postwar year," he remembers. "Some of us lived in what had been one of the school's tearooms, and we burned wood in open fires on the floor to get a little warmth."

During this postgraduate year he began to teach art at a public high school on a part-time basis, and when he had finished at Ueno he became a regular teacher. "Because I'm a print-maker, I suppose I've slanted my course toward *hanga*," he says. "My students are very enthusiastic about making prints, and they're doing fine work." Samples by seventh and eighth graders indicate that the standard is extraordinarily high in both black and white and color. Yoshida is proud of their work, proud that he is usually consulted on any international exchange of students' prints, and proud that, in a successful book on scenes of Tokyo illustrated by children, all but two or three of the prints were made in his classes.

Asked how he happened to turn to prints after starting out in oil, Yoshida replied that there were a number of reasons. "A minor one is that after the war the available oil paints were of very poor quality. More important, Kitaoka began to make prints in earnest and his work showed so much improvement over his oils that I couldn't help but be impressed. Furthermore, my own work was progressing toward the abstract and two dimensional, and I became convinced that for what I was trying to do the print is more suitable than oil." He pointed to some of his own abstract oil paintings in tones of grey, and to nearby prints in the same manner. "Those oil paintings fail completely—the whole effort comes perilously close to house painting—and yet in prints the same ideas are effective.

"I first became interested in abstract art at Ueno before the war. But it was Onchi, after the war, who gave me the impetus to do abstract work. Within the *Hanga* Association we set up a study group with Onchi as the leader. As I listened to him I found that he expressed many ideas I had long felt, and this gave me the confidence I needed.

"I'm the kind of artist who wants, not to develop new ideas, but to do something new. For many years my style was molded by reaction against my wartime experience. Life in the army was rough, confused, and violent. I'd had more than enough of that, but when I returned to Tokyo and went to see a large major exhibition I found that the whole show was battle itself. It set me to thinking. I wanted something orderly and serene and peaceful, and I decided on quiet greys in simple vertical and horizontal forms. My titles give a clue as to what I was seeking: some of my earliest work is a series called *Silence*.

"As I look back it's as though I had fled from the chaos of war to the peace and quiet of the desert. It was good for me, but after a while I needed something else and I left the desert for the forest. My new prints are conceived with a feeling of vigor and growth. From small prints I turned to big ones and from muted greys to the force of black and white. It was a major transition and it took me six months to resolve the design for the first one."

One of Yoshida's earlier prints is shown as print 84, and print 85 is one of his big new black and whites from the series *Fountain of Earth*. The new prints are made from single blocks of plywood and pose no technical problems, but for the older prints in grey it had been necessary to devise a new technique.

In cutting blocks the conventional way it is almost inevitable that there be either a slight overlap or a deliberate gap (Azechi, for example, has chosen the latter), but in Yoshida's prints in grey tones, any overlap or gap produced a new and unwanted form. His problem, then, was to achieve perfect registry, and his solution was one which Onchi described as "cut-out blocks." The blocks for these prints were made from solid *katsura*. Following the outlines of the design he had traced on the wood, Yoshida cut the board apart like a jigsaw puzzle, one piece for each form. He then mounted the assembled pieces in a frame, with backing, and to print any one form he raised it above the others by putting cardboard underneath it. For thin lines he printed from a strip of plastic inserted edgeways in a slot among his blocks.

He originated this technique not as a trick but because he wanted a clean line. It is not foolproof. There is the space left by the cut of the saw: the blocks must be just wet enough so that their swelling closes this gap. And with no margin for error he has to be particularly careful that his paper is evenly moistened: any irregular shrinkage as the paper dries will ruin the print. When he started he had a high percentage of failures, but now he has the method under control.

Technique, of course, is only a tool, but Yoshida used his new technique effectively. In his best prints in this style—for example, *Silence Number 50: Parting* (print 84), and *Peace-Evening*—the quiet tones and simple forms are amazingly evocative of the serenity he was seeking, and in this they must be counted as early successes.

His new prints burst the limits that he previously imposed upon himself and offer clear evidence that Yoshida is an artist of developing range and power. Since he is the kind of artist he is, it seems certain that these vigorous black and whites will in turn give way to something else as he follows his creed of probing the new. His should be an interesting career to watch.

FUMIO KITAOKA

Fumio Kitaoka (born 1918) was born in Tokyo of a well-to-do family. Like Yoshida, he studied cast drawing for a year at a private art school in preparation for the entrance examinations for the government art academy. There, in his last two years, he took Hiratsuka's course in print-making, and experienced, he says, "a childlike delight in carving the block and looking at the printed result."

Kitaoka graduated from Ueno at the same time as Yoshida, but unlike Yoshida, he was not immediately drafted, and he went to teach art at his former middle school. It was about this time that Hiratsuka, while on a trip to China and Manchuria, visited the headquarters of the East Asia Cultural Development Society, a semi-governmental agency designed to promote Japanese art in Manchuria. The society asked Hiratsuka to find them an artist to fill the position left vacant by Azechi, who had taught there for a year, and specified that they wanted someone skilled at figure drawing. Hiratsuka recalled that this was one of Kitaoka's strong points and recommended him. Kitaoka had just been married, but he went alone, and his bride joined him later.

With the end of the war and the shattering of Japan's Manchurian empire, the Kitaokas found themselves in a harsh world. "We Japanese refugees," he says, "were caught between the vicious bullying of the Chinese, Nationalist and Communist, and the cold indifference of our own Japanese officials who were running the refugee camps and arranging the long trip home. To complicate matters for my wife and me, it was then that our first daughter was born." There was seldom any transportation, and they had to walk most of the way, days over the mountains, weeks along the road, from one disordered camp to another, Kitaoka carrying their few belongings, and his wife, their baby.

Out of this experience came a series of compassionate prints called

152

Repatriation. "My principal reason for making these prints," says Kitaoka, "was not to portray the hardship we suffered, nor to protest against the evil we encountered, but to preserve the memory of our experience together and to try to express to my wife in my own way the gratitude that filled my heart."

In these black and white prints the influence of Hiratsuka is subordinated to that of Chinese realistic woodcuts. While he was stranded in Manchuria Kitaoka had met a Chinese whom he had known as a student at Ueno. Through his man he found some work doing woodcut illustrations for a Communist magazine, and he studied the technique of the simple, graphic Chinese prints. Later he helped introduce these prints to Japan, and found himself a hero among Japan's proletarian artists. "I soon recovered from this phase," he says, "because I was offended by both their doctrine and their method. I rebelled against their subjugation of art to politics, and I was repulsed by their barbarism and deliberate physical dirtiness.

"It was then I started to attend the Thursday-night meetings at Onchi's, for my interest was turning to an art of pure color and form. Onchi helped me to realize that pursuit of the sensitive, subtle beauty of these elements is the most exciting experience in art."

Kitaoka is now at the École des Beaux Arts in Paris. He is studying wood engraving, but he still prefers the Japanese-style block cut with the grain.

"I haven't given up painting," he says, "and I don't intend to, but prints have become my favorite medium. The colors come out more beautifully than anything done with a brush and the forms are clean-cut. Only the end results show, for all the pains taken to produce them are buried in prior work. I like prints, too, because when they are made the Japanese way, with *baren* and handmade paper, they are a very Japanese art, and it's good to feel at home in one's medium."

GEN YAMAGUCHI

The prints of Gen Yamaguchi (born 1903), like Onchi's, have frequently been made with leaves and other natural materials. "Onchi and I began almost simultaneously to make prints using natural objects," says Yamaguchi, "and although these were interesting experiments, I think now that we were getting too far from the basic element of wood. Besides, I want to develop continually as an artist rather than harden in any particular style." Yamaguchi's use of leaves is perhaps best seen in a pair of prints called *Poetry of Early Autumn* (one shown as print 83), while outstanding among his more recent prints are two called *Human Beings* (one shown as print 89) and an abstraction titled simply *Number 311*.

"I felt very close to Onchi," he says, "and I think that we shared many of the same attitudes, particularly towards printing. Most artists consider that the preparation of the block is the dominant activity, but Onchi found greater excitement in printing. His use of casual objects was in one way a de-emphasis of the block, his way of showing that, with creative printing, beauty could be realized from the most ordinary of blocks."

Yamaguchi, who is short, grey-haired, and square-jawed, with just a suggestion of the aesthete, lives in the fishing village of Enoura on the west coast of Izu Peninsula. He evacuated there from Tokyo late in the war, only to find that he was squarely in the course of the B-29's as they headed for the metropolis, but today it is peaceful, and when one has seen the view of sea and mountains from his upstairs studio it is easy to understand why he does not move back to the restless city.

He was born in Tokyo and went through middle school there without receiving any training in art. "Actually," he says, "I was more interested in literature when I was young, and if things had turned out differently, I might have been a writer today."

154

83. Poetry of Early Autumn (1947)   GEN YAMAGUCHI

He is a susceptible man, and his story reveals something of the intellectual and emotional currents that have swept Japan during his lifetime.

While still a child, he was captivated by the Sunday school conducted by a young missionary, and this early influence proved to be lasting, for he is still a Christian. Like many Japanese, he dislikes the alien formalism of church services, and he has found that it is not a simple matter to deal with the strains and tensions that arise from breaking with the family faith, but he has held to his religion quietly and unobtrusively.

As a young man he was attracted to the Shirakaba movement. This group came into the story of Un'ichi Hiratsuka and Takeo Takei through its work in introducing artists like Cezanne, Matisse, and van Gogh, but what excited young Yamaguchi was the "ideal village" then being promoted by one of the Shirakaba leaders, the author and painter Saneatsu Mushakoji. It was founded as a haven for writers and artists and conformed to the standard formula for such experiments: communal activity to provide food and shelter, and the rest of the time free for one's chosen work. Yamaguchi never joined the village, but he was intensely interested, and it was by reading everything that Mushakoji had written that he received his first background in art.

When he was about twenty he went along on one of his father's business trips to Formosa, where the family had prosperous beer and saké breweries. To escape the heat of Taipei some of his nostalgic countrymen had created in the mountains a typical Japanese hot-spring resort (it still exists, so much a thing apart that Japanese is even yet the language of the place), and here Yamaguchi met the early creative-print artist Shizuo Fujimori. Fujimori, a contemporary and close friend of Onchi's, was an oil painter who had turned to prints, but when Yamaguchi found him in Formosa he was more interested in collecting butterflies, and he promptly pressed the young man into service chasing over the hills after new specimens. Incidental to this athletic activity Yamaguchi succeeded in obtaining some lessons in print-making, and was able to produce a few prints himself.

Back in Japan several months later, he was impelled to a new group called Itto-en, which embodied a revolt against the materialism and intellectualism of the day. A quasi-philosophical movement with religious overtones, it was attracting a number of young writers and artists and, renouncing financial support from his family, Yamaguchi joined the brotherhood. As he describes it, they sheared their hair, wore a coarse, black kimono with a straw rope instead of the usual *obi* sash, and, barefooted, went out daily from their barracks to scourge themselves by hard work wherever they could find it. Since this was just after the earthquake of 1932, there was plenty to do. "We would go from house to house," he says, "offering our services at the back door. We would do any kind of work, no matter how dirty or unpleasant, and we kept our place as common laborers. We accepted no pay. If fed, we would eat; if not, we never asked."

Completely by accident, one of the houses he worked at was Koshiro Onchi's. "I didn't know it was Onchi's," Yamaguchi says. "I had misread the characters of the name painted on the gate." One day when he was taking a moment's rest, Onchi handed him a *hanga* magazine to look at; when he returned it Yamaguchi pointed to some work by Fujimori and quietly remarked that he knew him. The Onchis were already puzzled by the ascetic young man who asked for drudgery, and this statement deepened the mystery. They were no more perplexed than Fujmori, however, who turned up in due course and was nonplussed to find his well-to-do young friend from Formosa occupied in menial labor.

"After he understood," says Yamaguchi, "he introduced me to Onchi and told him about my interest in prints. Onchi didn't offer any encouragement, but he did say that the *Hanga* Association's annual show was coming up and asked me if I would donate my services to help with that. He gave me the job of registering the entries. When I looked at the very first print that came in I said to myself, 'I can do that,' and after work that evening I went back to the barracks and started a print. I finished in time to submit it to the show and it was accepted.

"It was a black and white, of course. I couldn't have made a color print so quickly, but most of the work then was in black and white, and overwhelmingly influenced by the Europeans. After all, this was the period when fashionable young artists drank no whisky but Scotch, used only French water colors, and painted with them on only English Waltman paper.

"I continued to visit Onchi and came to know other *hanga* artists, especially Azechi and Maeda, who have been close friends of mine ever since. I found myself increasingly preoccupied with art, and when some of my color prints were accepted for the next annual show I decided that the time had come for me to withdraw from Itto-en in order to study art.

"I excluded everything else from my life, even *hanga* and my *hanga* friends. I concentrated on sketching and water colors—oils were too expensive. Still, I was lucky compared with Azechi: my family was well off and could support me while I studied. I was strictly self-taught. I never even took my work to anyone for criticism."

Yamaguchi studied for about three years, and then, when one would expect his efforts to show results, he was again distracted by the turbulence of his age. The depression had set in and Japanese militarism was on the march, but countermovements were still fighting back. "I never was a Communist," says Yamaguchi, "but I was —I am—a liberal, and I fought militarism as long as it could be fought." He doesn't talk about these years of his life, and even friends as close as Onchi never learned exactly what he did; he simply disappeared. "It was about 1937," he continues, "when the fight was about over and lost, that I met Azechi quite accidentally in the galleries at Ueno. It had been a long time, and he said they all had wondered what had become of me. He reminded me that the *Hanga* Association still held shows and asked me to participate again. I did, and I've been active ever since.

"I resumed my association with Onchi and moved into a house near his. Sekino then lived in the same neighborhood, and it was our almost daily visits to Onchi that developed into the Ichimoku-kai sessions.

"Those were exciting and fruitful meetings," he says. "Onchi

157

GEN YAMAGUCHI

was a great leader, but he never dominated. He didn't like disciple relationships. He would give everything that was in him to someone who was prepared to receive, but he never tried to give anything to someone who wasn't ready. In this respect he stood somewhere between Maekawa, who will have nothing to do with teaching, and Hiratsuka, who will take a student by the hand whether he is ready to learn or not.

"What Onchi taught me was the attitude of an artist, the attitude becoming to an artist. I remember that years earlier I had seen an old, cracked tile. I thought it was beautiful and wondered why such elements couldn't be incorporated in art. In Onchi's work I found acceptance of this and much more, and a door was opened for me.

"Onchi was a vital artist and he was impatient with talk of theory, but he had theory, and he had the inspiration and passion of a great artist. He was the embodiment of modern *hanga* in Japan and our ambassador to the rest of the world. He was heart and mind, and how we miss him!"

84. *Silence Number 50: Parting (1953)*

MASAJI
YOSHIDA

85. *Fountain of Earth: Number 1 (1956)*

86. *Ships at Rest* (1952)

FUMIO KITAOKA

87. *Still Life on a Table* (1948)

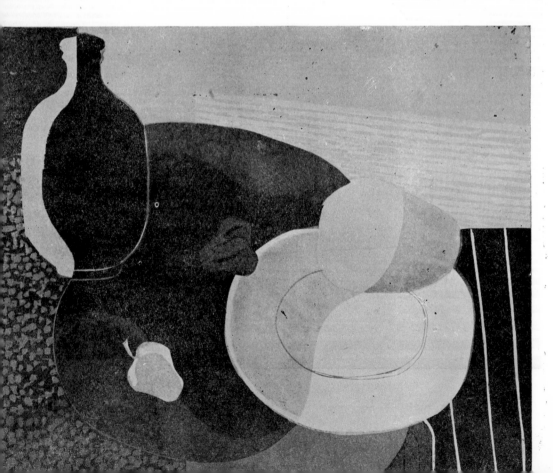

GEN
YAMAGUCHI

88. *Window (1948)*

89. *Human Beings (1953)*

14
OTHER CURRENTS

Tomoo Inagaki
Kihei Sasajima
The Yoshida Family
Thoru Mabuchi

IN TELLING THE STORY OF THESE MEN IT HAS BEEN NOTED THAT MANY OF them became print artists with very little formal training either in art or in their chosen medium. That they should have turned to prints, that over three hundred artists are active in *sosaku hanga* today, shows both the strength of the movement and the Japanese familiarity with *hanga*. It goes without saying that the Japanese have known prints long and intimately, for until not so long ago they were the only convenient means of publishing a picture or a text. Being familiar with prints does not necessarily lead to making them, but the Japanese have always been closer to the practice of art than most Westerners, largely because of their use of the brush in calligraphy and their regard for calligraphy as an art. The *sosaku* artists have done their part, too, for they have enthusiastically advocated *hanga* as a hobby, and by their books and articles, courses and study groups, have done all they could to give the public both the urge to make prints and the basic knowledge of how to go about it. An annual contest to choose the best self-made New Year's card now draws

163

thousand of submissions. It all adds up to the fact that the woodblock is a medium that the Japanese feels at home in, one that he is likely to turn to for artistic expression.

No common bond of approach links the artists discussed in this chapter, but each of them is doing work that merits inclusion in this introduction to creative *hanga*. Some of them became print artists in their maturity and some were born to prints, but they all feel at home with them.

TOMOO INAGAKI

For his start in prints Tomoo Inagaki (born 1902) looks back to a magazine published by Onchi and Hiratsuka in the early 1920's, *Poems and Hanga*. Contributions in both fields were invited from the readers, and Inagaki, only a few years out of high school, had a print accepted. He was then eligible to attend the "family meetings," in which the editors and contributors discussed common problems and criticized each other's work.

"I owe a great deal to *Poems and Hanga*," he says. "I became a regular contributor and attended the meetings religiously. I learned a lot from those meetings—they were my only training in woodblocks, and a very important part of my total training in art—and I made lifelong friendships with men like Susumu Yamaguchi." Shizuo Fujimori, who figured in Gen Yamaguchi's career, was also connected with the magazine, and later Inagaki studied drawing from him in a Sunday class. "I like some qualities and reject others in Matisse and Piccaso," he says, "but, above all, I was influenced by Onchi and Hiratsuka." To demonstrate, he laughingly displays two early prints, one in his Onchi style, and one in the Hiratsuka manner, both very neat imitations.

Slender, long-haired Inagaki was born and brought up in Tokyo

90. *Cat Making Up (1955)*   TOMOO INAGAKI

and attended a commercial high school. After graduation he went to work for a steel company, but the pull toward art, which had caused him to try oil paintings while going to school and prints later, proved too strong. *"Poems and Hanga* convinced me," he says, "that I wanted to be a print artist. Common sense told me I couldn't make a living at it, but by then I knew that steel was not for me, so I quit my job and enrolled in a commercial-art school." Following his two-year course, he worked for a few months in the display department of a Yokohama store, and then set up his own commercial-art studio in downtown Tokyo. He ran his own business until the war and bombings made the location unhealthy, and since then he has done free-lance design, with some teaching on the side.

Cats are one of his favorite subjects, and among his best prints are *Cat Making Up* (print 90), *Walking Cat,* and *Cat on a Chair,* the latter featuring an imperious white creature, Inagaki's own, surveying his domain from a blue cushion. Among his other outstanding prints are *Lamp* (print 91), *Chrysanthemum, Flower in a Black Vase,* and *Record of My Crop* (print 92).

In color Inagaki tends toward the very characteristic Japanese color scheme of black and brown, the latter sometimes brightened by orange. In carving he uses almost the full range of tools but with emphasis on the flat chisels. "It's easier to develop a distinctive style by restricting yourself to certain tools," he says, "but I don't want to limit myself that way."

He does not make detailed sketches for his prints. From rough drafts he lays out a full-scale design in pencil. He goes over this with brush and *sumi,* and then, laying it face down on a wet block, he rubs with a *baren* to transfer the *sumi* to the board and give him his plan for carving, a plan he frequently revises as he works. For small prints he uses solid *katsura* or occasionally *ho,* but he carves his large prints on plywood faced with *shina.*

Just after the war the shortage of good wood and paper started him making pictures with stencils, but now that fine materials are again available he uses stencils only occasionally.

KIHEI
SASAJIMA

Kihei Sasajima (born 1906) considers Munakata his teacher. "Munakata is a genius," he says, "but so unique that I don't suppose he will ever command a wide influence. I'm continually amazed at his work, at its size and scale and force. He awes me. When I learned that he had won the 1955 prize for prints at Sao Paulo I knew I should go and congratulate him in person but I'm afraid to see him. He's too overwhelming. I thought about it a long time, but I finally wrote a letter instead."

Sasajima, who resembles George Arliss in the role of Disraeli, was born about eighty-five miles north of Tokyo in the pottery town of Mashiko, where his father was a local politician. Sasajima loved to draw, but there was no chance for training until he came to Tokyo to go to teacher's college, and there took a course in sketching. "Immediately," he says, "I fell in love with art."

After he finished college he started teaching in elementary schools, work he kept up until 1945, and in his free time he studied oils and drawing. His first real contact with print-making came in 1935 when he attended a course for teachers given by Hiratsuka.

"Just before that I had become deeply interested in calligraphy," he says, "so I was prepared for composition in black and white. Besides, while I was teaching, my only free time was at night, and black and white is best when it is necessary to work under artificial light."

Hiratsuka's instruction had been germinating three or four years when Sasajima decided he wanted to make prints. When he talked it over with Shoji Hamada, the great *mingei* potter who had settled in Mashiko, Hamada told him that he ought to go see Munakata, and he did. "Munakata is not a very good teacher," says Sasajima, "but I absorbed a great deal from him. My problem now is to stand on my own. I want to try to find a Japanese expression for the Japanese. It's lamentable that everybody is traveling along the

166

same path. You can't tell whether much of the work is done by a Japanese or a Westerner.

"I want to get away from the perspective and third dimension that I have been using and try to achieve the two dimensional quality of calligraphy," he goes on. "Scale is more important than superficial depth."

Sasajima has made some small color prints, usually restricting himself to three or four colors, but most of his work is in black and white. He uses a line that is longer than Hiratsuka's and closer to the brush stroke. He believes that this has been derived from his study of Munakata, calligraphy, and the *nanga* painters of both China and Japan, especially Taiga and Tessai.

His best prints are landscapes, and while they do not have the tension and solid construction of Hiratsuka's, most of them have a lightness and a graciousness which give them an immediate appeal. Representative examples are *Early Winter in the Mountains* (print 93), *A Mountain Stream* (print 94), *A Hill in Early Spring*, and *Hatagaya Landscape*.

"The Yoshida Family" (no relation to Masaji Yoshida already discussed) is a convenient tag for what is almost a one-family art movement. The first artist of the family was Kosaburo Yoshida, whose work illustrates the Italian influence in Japanese art. In the 1870's the Japanese government established its first school to teach Western art and, turning to Europe for the staff, recruited a number of Italian artists. One of these was Antonio Fontanesi, and Kosaburo studied with him.

Among Kosaburo's children was his daughter Fujio (born 1887), whose masculine-sounding name still causes confusion. It seemed for many years that Kosaburo's offspring were going to be restricted to daughters; so he adopted a son, the promising young man who became Hiroshi Yoshida (1876–1950). Things turned out well, for Hiroshi achieved not one but two careers in art, first as an oil painter, then a print artist. Moreover, he and Fujio, an artist her-

YOSHIDA
FAMILY

self, were married, and their two sons, Toshi (born 1911) and Hodaka (born 1926), constitute the third generation of Yoshida artists, while Toshi's sons show possibilities of being the fourth.

Hiroshi Yoshida is a prominent figure in modern Japanese prints, but his work was not in the field of creative *hanga*. However, when midway in his career he decided to switch from oils to prints, he became his own publisher, and the best carvers and printers he could find worked in his studio under his personal supervision. In addition, he thoroughly mastered the techniques himself, so that when he felt the occasion demanded he could carve a troublesome portion of a block, or show how he wanted it printed. This might appear to be a long step toward creative prints, but it was more a return to the best practices of *ukiyoe*, when the artist, if he were blessed with a conscientious publisher, could, at least in the first edition, carefully direct the artisans. Hiroshi had more than technique in common with *ukiyoe*, for he shared its artistic approach as well, and in all respects held a point of view at odds with that of the *sosaku* artists.

His sons grew up in the studio, surrounded by print-making. While he was still a boy, Toshi showed promise of becoming an artist, and in addition to the training he absorbed by watching the artisans, his father started teaching him when he was fourteen. At twenty he began the four-year course at the Taiheiyo art school, a private school operated by the Taiheiyo Art Association. His father had helped found both, and was a member of the school's faculty.

Toshi's first prints were extremely close to his father's in style, and made by artisans, but in the meantime he was exploring new avenues in his oils. "My father loved the mountains," he says, "so I turned to the sea." First came a series of underwater scenes, and then a group of paintings inspired by microscopic examination of the life that swarms in a drop of sea water. On Toshi's canvases tiny plankton were hugely magnified and given a color scheme of his own invention, for under the microscope he found them uniformly grey.

"From these paintings it was an easy—I suppose inevitable—step to abstraction," says Toshi, "but it was a step my father could never approve. Still, I could not ignore the movement of the times and I began to break away from my former realistic approach two or three years after the war."

He still makes some prints almost indistinguishable from his father's, but these are studio prints carved and printed by artisans, though, like his father, he may occasionally help with the carving or printing of one. Like Tokuriki, he keeps his *sosaku* prints quite apart. Many of the latter are based on a bold simplification of natural forms, but he has often gone beyond this to abstraction. His subjects often reflect his travels, as his father's prints did before him, and range from an *Arab of Bagdad* to the *American Girl* and from an *Evening in Venice* to the *Indian Village, New Mexico* (print 95).

Hodaka, born fifteen years after Toshi and named after one of his father's favorite mountains (see Susumu Yamaguchi's print 69), was not supposed to be an artist. He painted as a child, then stopped, and his father, deciding that he was meant for a career in science, enrolled him in a preparatory course leading to a university education in that field. It was a three-year course, but it took Hodaka five, for midway in the course his interest in art suddenly revived and he started painting again. His work was completely abstract, and guilty not only of that but also of painting when he was supposed to be studying science, he found it expedient to paint in the attic and hide his canvases there until time to smuggle them out for exhibition. None of this trickery increased his father's admiration for his work, but Hodaka achieved some measure of satisfaction when one of his attic abstractions won a prize in a Tai-heiyo show, a prize his father was obligated to present.

"My father's opposition made me an abstract artist," he says. "I've always liked Miro and Klee, but I don't know that either has been a concrete influence. Lately I've turned to traditional Japanese art.

"At first I did almost no prints, though of course I'd been steeped in the technique since I was a child. I started to make prints around 1950, and I've carved and printed my own from the beginning." Among his most interesting prints are *Woods, Night,* and *Buddhist Statues* (print 97). He has also experimented with a combination of woodblock and dry point, an improvised technique in which he makes the block by scratching his design on celluloid.

Chizuko Yoshida (born 1924), slim, pert, and vivacious, is a Yoshida by marriage, Hodaka's wife. "I liked art from my kindergarten days," she says. "I studied water colors in high school, and after high school I started to study oil with Kitaoka. That was when he had just finished at Ueno and before he left for Manchuria, and since he was doing prints as well as oils, I was exposed to them, too. Later I went to the Hongo art school until it burned in the air raids, and then I evacuated to Aomori. I did some sketching in Aomori but I spent more time practicing the violin."

After the war she returned to Tokyo, resumed her painting, and began submitting work to the Taiheiyo shows. In 1949 she was made an associate member of the group. That was the year that Hodaka won his prize, and it was then they became acquainted.

With prints in the air as they are at the Yoshidas' it was inevitable that she should start making them. "I want to make it very clear," she says with wifely concern, "that it was Hodaka who was my teacher in prints." She admits, however, that she is probably further from traditional technique than anyone else in the family,

170

and she attributes this to learning the use of plywood and string from Kitaoka.

Shortly before they were married, she and Hodaka attended a few of Onchi's Ichimoku-kai sessions. "We only got in on the last of those meetings," she says, "but even so, they, and Onchi, were stimulating. I wish we could have started earlier."

Chizuko's work shows a marked musical influence, and some of her prints, like the series called *Jazz,* even bear musical titles. Others, like *Sounds in the Night* and *Frozen* (print 98), suggested by cracking ice, seem to appeal to the ear as well as the eye. Music is important to her: she plays the violin, likes opera, and, she confesses with a quick smile, "I sing when I work."

The newest addition to the Yoshida print-makers is the oldest member of the group, Fujio, Hiroshi's widow. She has been an active artist all of her life, managing to exhibit even in the years when she relegated art to a hobby in order to raise her children, but only in recent years has she seriously tackled prints.

Describing her husband's change from oils to prints she recalls the trip they made to America in 1923. "We started in December after the earthquake," she says. "In addition to my husband's paintings we took the work of a number of other artists, trying to help some of those who had lost almost everything in the disaster. We had shows in several major cities, but we sold discouragingly few pictures. There was a good deal more interest in a few prints that my husband had taken along—his first prints, commissioned and published by the house of Watanabe. The fine reception given these prints, plus the fact that several foreign print-artists had recently created a stir in Japan, made my husband think that the Japanese had better get busy in the field that was once their own, and he started concentrating on prints as soon as we returned. It was then he decided to become his own publisher."

171

Mrs. Yoshida tried designing a few artisan prints in 1926, and then went back to her painting. "Most of my work has been realistic," she says. "It wasn't until about 1946 that I started making 'queer pictures.' Like Toshi, I couldn't ignore the movement of the times." Her "queer pictures," like *Myoga* (print 96), are mostly of flowers, great enlargements catching the swirl of color and form in the central structure. In 1953 she designed such a print for artisan production, and the next year, at the age of sixty-seven, she started to carve her own blocks and do her own printing. "It's an exciting and challenging field," she says, "and I like it."

The Yoshidas' creative prints are made on the same fine paper they use for their studio prints, a special *kizuki hosho* from Echizen and, following the size limitations of that paper, are somewhat smaller than the major work of most *sosaku* artists. Their work with artisans has influenced them in other ways, too, for it has given them a respect for paper and pigment which some of the other artists lack, and given their printing a kind of clean, craftsman quality which few of the other artists seem interested in. It is this technically conservative approach which sets them a little apart, and makes them distinctive in *sosaku hanga*.

THORU MABUCHI

Thoru Mabuchi (born 1920) was intended for the career of an artist even before he was born. (The spelling of his given name is his own: it would commonly be romanized as Toru.) An artist's career had been his father's dream for himself, but thrown on his own when he was very young, the problems of making a living had shouldered the dream aside. He had turned to commercial art, but because of his own frustrated ambitions, he and his wife agreed that if their first child were a boy he would be sent to art school and given the chance denied his father. In this case it all worked out as it was supposed to, contrary to the usual tendency of sons to upset the plans their fathers make for them.

His father had been a cut-grain wood engraver when that technique monopolized illustration in Japan but, having seen that the advent of photoengraving spelled doom to his trade, had been one of the first in Japan to take up the airbrush in the field of commercial art. He had been a real pioneer, learning the technique from French and American books, and designing his own airbrush to be made locally. It was not easy to promote the new idea, but inevitably it caught on, and he has had his own commercial-art studio ever since.

Giving up his wood engraving as a business, he continued it as a hobby, and his son learned by watching him. Never permitted to use his father's tools, Thoru bought his own out of his allowance, and as early as grammar school he was making prints, mostly greeting cards, with which he deluged his friends.

When he had finished the elementary grades, his parents moved so he could go to a middle school which would prepare him for art school. Here his incipient career almost foundered, for Mabuchi, a big man now and a husky boy then, attracted much too favorable attention in the military drills which in those days were a standard part of the curriculum. As a result, his instructor, a navy reservist, recommended him for a government naval academy and informed him that his future lay with the navy. Mabuchi was not enthusiastic but didn't see that he had much choice in the matter, and with a naval career looming, he began neglecting his art. When this became evident at home, his worried mother went to see his art teacher, who thereupon called the boy in and sternly rebuked him for not working at his art when he was destined for art school. Such a reprimand carries a good deal more weight in Japan than it might elsewhere, and despite the objections of the military instructor, Mabuchi mended his ways. Filial duty was then still an overriding virtue in Japan.

"After middle school, I entered the design course in the government art school at Ueno," he says. "This course included oil painting and drawing, but it emphasized the decorative and applied arts. My

173

father wanted me to be an artist, but he wanted me to be able to earn a living too.

"I kept up my work in prints while I was in school, and in my last two years, when a student is allowed to exhibit, I showed prints in some of the major exhibitions. Then too as an advanced student I was able to enter Hiratsuka's class, and he gave me criticism outside of class as well. Actually, I had absorbed from my father most of what Hiratsuka was teaching, but hearing it from Hiratsuka strengthened my technique and gave me confidence. The technique of every creative-print artist differs, a point that Hiratsuka himself emphasizes, but it's helpful to know how another man works.

"I sketch in oils, water colors, and pastels, but I've never exhibited anything but prints, and I think of myself as a print artist. For my graduation thesis I did a series of twelve prints which I called *An Interpretation of Nature in Woodprints.* I think it's the only time a student at Ueno has made prints for his thesis." It must be noted that Mabuchi's being in the design course gave him a certain latitude with respect to medium, and made possible such a deviation from the school's normal requirements.

He graduated in December 1941 and immediately was taken into the army. Here his physique again made him stand out: he was picked for the regiment assigned to guard the Imperial Palace and sat out the war in Tokyo. "It wasn't long before they learned about my art training," says Mabuchi, "and I spent the war making maps and charts. I never had to carry a rifle.

"As soon as the war was over, I started to take over my father's office. He still works there, and so do my two younger brothers, but the management of the office is now my responsibility."

As might be expected from his background, Mabuchi is a fine technician, and because of his competence and assurance he is inclined to more elaborate printing than is usual in creative *hanga,* some of his prints running from thirty to fifty printing stages. He is unwilling to limit himself to traditional technique. "I want to make prints which are unlike prints," he says. "Like Saito, I want to get away from the traditional." Two of his long-time interests probably determined his course: the Byzantine mosaics and the

174

pointillist paintings of Seurat. These enthusiasms led Mabuchi to develop a technique in which he makes his blocks by cutting small pieces of thin wood and gluing them to a board. There is no similarity to Masaji Yoshida's "cut-out blocks," for Mabuchi's small pieces are like the stones of a mosaic, whereas Yoshida's blocks are the actual shape of his forms.

"I started by attempting the pointillist technique of juxtaposing spots of primary colors, but it didn't work," he says, " so I fell back on the mosaic effect." In his first attempt he cut up a wooden box of the kind used by the Japanese as single-use lunch boxes, dedicating it to art after he had eaten his lunch. Now he uses the thin strips of wood used by printers to space out their lines of type. He makes several blocks and prints from them in the conventional way. "The jury at the government show always argues about accepting these prints," he says, " because the blocks aren't carved, but so far they've been accepted."

Thus far he has concentrated on landscapes, and whether by carved or mosaic blocks, his prints tend to be large and boldly designed. Among the best are *Mountain Lake* (print 99), *Kilns at Mashiko,* and *Afternoon Sun* (print 100).

Mabuchi is still young, and he lays out his plans this way: "I want to do something that only a Japanese can do, something rooted in Japanese tradition. Even if someday I'm able to tour and sketch in foreign countries, I want my pictures to be recognizably the work of a Japanese.

"People tried to make a universal language of Esperanto, but they failed. I don't believe that a universal language in art would be any more successful than Esperanto. Art is universal, but each country should have its own expression, and I want to contribute to Japan's."

91. *Lamp (1954)*

TOMOO
INAGAKI

92. *Record of My
Crop (1949)*

93. *Early Winter in the Mountains (1947)*

KIHEI SASAJIMA

94. *A Mountain Stream (1954)*

95. Toshi Yoshida:
*Indian Village,
New Mexico*
(1955)

THE
YOSHIDA
FAMILY

96. Fujio Yoshida:
Myoga (1954)

97. Hodaka Yoshida:
Buddhist Statues
(1954)

98. Chizuko Yoshida:
Frozen (1955)

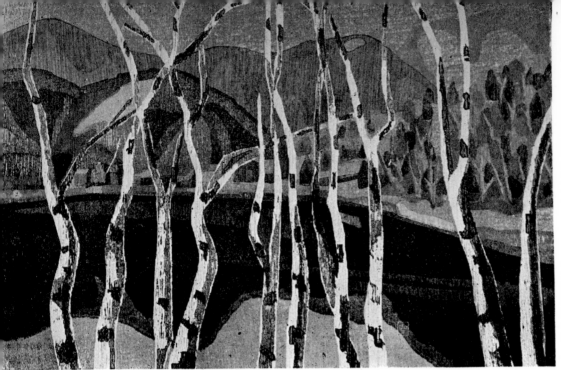

99. *Mountain Lake (1954)*

THORU MABUCHI

100. *Afternoon Sun (1953)*

EPILOGUE

THIS HAS BEEN AN INTRODUCTION TO A LIVING ART, YOUNG, EVOLVING, AND spirited. An international heritage has given it vitality; deep roots in the past have given it strength.

From old ways and new ideas, Japanese prints have been reborn. It is not fifty years since Kanae Yamamoto came back from a seaside holiday with a new vision of an old medium. Almost three-fourths of the prints shown in these pages are less than ten years old.

Even before this book is published some one of these artists may have struck out on a new course which will throw his whole career into a different focus. Some one of them may have produced new work towering over everything he did before. And in one of the tiny galleries that crowd the map of Tokyo, an even happier event may have occurred: some unheralded young artist may emerge with new prints of force and beauty. For this is a living art. It is good that the story can be left unfinished.

APPENDIX I: THE WOODS

Throughout the text the woods used by the artists to make the blocks for their prints are referred to by their common Japanese names. Below is a table which shows the scientific and common English name for each wood, with a brief statement of the characteristics which relate to its use in making printing blocks. Most of the information is taken from a report prepared by the Natural Resources Section, General Headquarters, Supreme Commander for the Allied Powers, Tokyo, 1951.

Japanese Name	Scientific Name	English Name	Characteristics
Buna 橅	Fagus crenata Bl.	Siebold's beech	Fine texture and straight grain; heavy, tough, and relatively hard.
Hō 朴	Magnolia obovata Thunb.	Silver magnolia	Very fine texture and straight grain; light, soft, and flexible.
Katsura 桂	Cercidiphyllum japonicum S. et Z.	Katsura	Fine, uniform texture and straight grain; low shrinkage or swelling with change in moisture content; light, soft, and very easy to work.
Keyaki 欅	Zelkova serrata Mak.	Zelkova	One of Japan's finest furniture hardwoods; coarse structure and straight, handsome grain; heavy and hard, but easy to work; unique to Japan and the Ryukyus.
Rawan ラワン	Shorea negrosensis Foxw. and Pentacme contorta Merr. et Rolf.	Lauan	An imported wood, one of the Philippine mahoganies; medium texture and straight grain; a medium weight hardwood; easy to work.
Sakura 櫻	Prunus spp.	Cherry	Fine texture and straight, sometimes figured grain; medium heavy and moderately hard; easily worked; little tendency to warp, and low shrinkage or swelling with change in moisture content; the wood usually used for traditional ukiyoe.
Shina 科	Tilia japonica Simk.	Basswood; Japanese linden	Fine texture and straight grain; light, soft, and easily worked.
Yanagi 柳	Salix spp.	Willow	Fine texture and close, straight grain; very light, soft, and easy to work.

APPENDIX 2: THE PRINTS

The following is general and technical information concerning the prints reproduced. In most cases it was obtained from the artist, often with mutual examination of his blocks, his notes, and his working sketches.

Such information about Kanae Yamamoto's prints is limited, because the artist himself is usually the only reliable source. The specific information given for each of his prints was obtained from colleagues and contemporary periodicals and catalogues. In addition, the following is generally true. Date: it is believed that prints signed "Kanae" in roman letters are later prints and were made in Japan. Edition: no accurate information could be obtained; however, before Yamamoto left for Paris a subscription series had been arranged, and several of the smaller prints made in Europe were for this series; the number of subscribers is not known, but the distribution of these prints must have been relatively wide, perhaps 25–50. Blocks: Yamamoto's training as a wood engraver accustomed him to using *sakura* blocks, and most of his prints were made with *sakura;* it is believed that he used some *ho* but no *katsura;* prints made in Europe were carved on Japanese blocks, which he either took with him or had sent to him. Pigment: usually French water colors, although he took to Europe a supply of the Japanese blue vegetable pigment called *ai,* and in prints made in Japan he is thought to have used *sumi* for his blacks. Paper: the paper used for each print has been identified, and it may be noted that Yamamoto used Japanese paper for all of his European prints.

The term "printing stages" as used throughout the appendix may require a little explanation. It is used to indicate the number of steps in the printing in which a new element in the design or coloring is introduced; it does not refer to the number of times the artist presses the paper to the block, for he may do this several times in one printing stage in order to obtain depth of color. A single block, however, may incorporate several printing stages: different portions of the block may be used separately, or the same portion more than once, with different colors.

FRONTISPIECE. Koshiro Onchi: *Impression of a Violinist.* Polychrome impression, 16×12 3/4 in. Published in 1947. Carved, printed, and published by the artist. Edition: 13 (Onchi planned an edition of 20 and numbered his prints accordingly, but never completed the edition); in addition, since Onchi's death, the professional printer Koichi Hirai has been commissioned to print an indefinite number as a memorial edition. Blocks: 2 blocks of solid *katsura;* 3 printing stages. Pigment: poster colors. Paper: *torinoko.* Location: Honolulu Academy of Arts and the collection of the author. Notes: Onchi made this print after hearing a concert by Nejiko Suwa, as told in the text. He also wrote a companion poem, dated October 29, 1947, which has been translated as follows (the reader will note the emphasis on yellow; Onchi originally made the violinist's face yellow but quickly eliminated this touch):

Impression of a Violinist

The bow rises strongly into the air.
The artificial lights turned on this
  violinist's slender body,
How yellow they seem!—
On her pale face, on the white silk.
This body passed through a Europe
  torn with war,
And stands now on the stage of an
  occupied country.
Ah, the sounds of rubbing strings keep
  gnawing at one's heart,
How sad a thing art is!
My heart turns yellow,
My tears turn yellow too.

The frontispiece to this book was made available through the kindness of Toyohisa Adachi and the Adachi Institute of Woodcut Prints. To make this reproduction Hanbei Okura carved 5 blocks of solid *katsura;* 3 of the blocks were carved from a photograph pasted to the block, and the other 2 blocks were carved by an *ukiyoe* technique known as *mudabori:* certain areas already carved on one of the first 3 blocks were recarved on new blocks. For example, the mouth was carved originally on one of the first 3 blocks; an impression was struck off from this block and pasted to a new block as a guide; the mouth was carved on the new block and then cut off the original block (since the mouth is printed with a different color it simplifies printing to have it on a separate block, not too close to other color areas). Four printers (Wasakichi Komatsu, Hatsutaro Kinoshita, Shunosuke Fujii, and Shinzo Toyoda) worked as a team to do the printing in 6 stages, each man working with a different block or blocks. The pigments used were *sumi* (for the grey and black), *beni* (for the red of the mouth), and *benigara* (for the brown of the violin); the *beni* and *benigara* are mineral pigments, not the vegetable colors of the same name which were used to make old *ukiyoe* prints. The paper is white *torinoko* from Echizen.

DEDICATION PAGE. Jun'ichiro Sekino: *Koshiro Onchi.* Polychrome impression, 24 1/2 × 18 3/4 in. Published in 1952. Carved, printed, and published by the artist. Edition: limited to 30 (about 15 printed to date). Blocks: 8 blocks of plywood faced with *shina;* 23 printing stages, including one for the string in the design of the print Onchi is holding. Pigment: both liquid and chalk *sumi,* tube water colors for the face and hands, gouache for the other colors. Paper: *torinoko.* Location: Art Institute of Chicago. Notes: Sekino says that in early 1952 he made several sketches for this portrait, but that none were very satisfactory because Onchi quickly tired of posing and usually ended up trying to sketch Sekino. Sekino adds that he purposely deformed Onchi's face into a crescent in order to catch his character and to fit the pictorial design. Onchi is holding one of his own prints, but Sekino unintentionally modified the design. In order to show the print as it would look from the back, Sekino printed it with a tissue between the blocks and the paper. The string design above the circle in the print Onchi holds is printed from freely formed actual string and hence is different in each impression.

1. Kanae Yamamoto: *On the Deck.* Polychrome impression, 6 7/8 × 6 5/8 in. Published about 1912. Carved, printed, and published by the artist. Edition: not known, but this print was one of the subcription series. Paper: *nishinouchi,* a pure *kozo* paper in a fine, thin grade. Location: collection of the author. Notes: It is believed that Yamamoto made this print early in his stay in Paris from sketches made during the voyage there; at least some of the blocks were probably carved during the voyage.

2. ——: *A Small Bay in Brittany.* Polychrome impression, 5 5/16 × 8 1/2 in. Published about 1913. Carved, printed, and published by the artist. Edition: not known, but this print was one of the subscription series. Paper: *nishinouchi,* same as for *On the Deck.* Location: Mr. S. Nakajima, Tokyo. Notes: This print is believed to have been made early in his stay in France.

3. ———: *Fisherman*. Polychrome impression, 6 7/16 × 4 3/8 in. Published in 1904. Carved, printed, and published by the artist. Blocks: two blocks of solid *sakura*. Location: no copy of the original print is known to exist. Notes: This is the print which Tsuruzo Ishii describes as the first creative print made in Japan (see text). The reproduction here is taken from the reproduction in the July 1, 1904, issue of the art and poetry magazine *Myojo*, where it is listed as a *toga* (knife picture). The measurements given above are the measurements of the reproduction in *Myojo*, but that reproduction is believed to have been printed from the original blocks. In a feature called "Palette Diary" in the same issue Hakutei Ishii made the following comment under the date June 16: "Friend Kanae Yamamoto combines his artistic talent and cut-grain wood-engraving technique to make an artist's wood print. The knife is the brush. It is illustrated in this issue." The reproduction herein was photographed from the files of *Myojo* in the National Library, Ueno, Tokyo, and the seal of the library can be seen extending from the left center margin.

4. ———: *French Pastoral in Spring*. Polychrome impression, 9 3/4 × 13 1/4 in. Published about 1913. Carved, printed, and published by the artist. Paper: *nishinouchi,* same as for *On the Deck*. Location: collection of the author.

5. ———: *Woman of Brittany*. Polychrome impression, 14 1/2 × 11 1/4 in. Published in 1920. Carved, printed, and published by the artist. Blocks: solid *sakura,* number not known. Paper: *kizuki hosho,* a fine, thin grade, pure *kozo*. Location: collection of the author. Notes: This print was made at Oya, in Shinshu.

6. ———: *Moscow Street*. Polychrome impression, 5 1/4 × 5 11/16 in. Published about 1916. Carved, printed, and published by the artist. Paper: *nishinouchi,* same as for print 7. Location: collection of the author. Notes: There are those who believe that Yamamoto made this print in Moscow, others that he made it just after his return to Japan.

7. ———: *Moscow*. Polychrome impression, 13 1/2 × 16 1/2 in. Published about 1917. Carved, printed, and published by the artist. Edition: this was a subscription print; about 30 were made for subscribers, plus about 10 so-called "test runs" for friends. Blocks: 8 blocks of solid *sakura;* these are the blocks that have survived (see text); they consist of 4 boards, each carved on both sides; a contemporary artist who examined the blocks identified at least 19 printing stages. Paper: *nishinouchi,* a fine but somewhat heavier grade than *On the Deck*. Location: collection of the author. Notes: It is believed that this was among the first prints Yamamoto made after his return from Europe and that he made it at Oya, in Shinshu.

8. Koshiro Onchi: *Objet Number 2*. Polychrome impression, 22 1/2 × 16 3/4 in. Published in 1954. Carved, printed, and published by the artist. Edition: 3. Blocks: 8 blocks of *tsuge* (boxwood) and *matsu* (pine), 14 blocks of charcoal; 22 printing stages. Pigment: gouache for the wood blocks and poster color for the red of the charcoal blocks. Paper: *torinoko*. Location: Honolulu Academy of Arts and collection of the author. Notes: Onchi picked up the wooden blocks for this print from scraps left when a house was built for his daughter and her husband. The charcoal blocks were made from pieces of ordinary charcoal, cut through the middle so as to reveal the inner structure, and printed one at a time. This print is one of a series of designs numbered as "Objets."

9. ———: *Among the Rocks*. Polychrome impression, 19 5/8 × 14 1/2 in. Published in 1929. Carved, printed, and published by the artist. Edition: 3. Blocks: 6 blocks of solid *katsura;* 13 printing stages. Pigment: water colors, poster colors, and oil paints. Paper: *torinoko*. Location: collection of the author. Notes: This print shows Onchi's two sons playing among the rocks at the seashore.

10. ———: *Portrait of Sakutaro Hagiwara*. Polychrome impression, 20 3/4 × 16 3/8 in. Published in 1943. Carved, printed, and published by the artist. Edition: 7 (50

additional copies were printed from Onchi's blocks by Jun'ichiro Sekino in 1949, and since Onchi's death Koichi Hirai has been commissioned to print an indefinite number as a memorial edition). Blocks: 7 blocks of solid *katsura;* 15 printing stages. Pigment: *sumi,* water colors, and poster colors. Paper: *edogawa* and different types of *torinoko* (see text). Location: Museum of Fine Arts, Boston; Honolulu Academy of Arts; and the collection of the author. Notes: This print is also reproduced in *The Floating World* and Michener gives a vivid description of its creation. Hagiwara, one of Onchi's close friends, was a nihilistic poet who was born in 1886 and died in 1942, crushed by the tragedy of his era. Onchi (who called this portrait *The Author of "The Ice Island,"* taking his title from one of Hagiwara's major works) also wrote the following poem, dated September 23, 1947, about his friend:

The Author of "The Ice Island"

Words vault over words and emotions turn somersault,
Life loses its footing and the spirit tumbles down.
Even a single truth becomes covered with a veil of sham.
The foolish retina quite diffuses the light,
Words are but reflections,
Verse is victimized by words.
Poetry, too, is falsehood.
(Sakutaro grasped "nothingness" from this falsehood, grasped it as he would a dream.)
Emotions turn somersault and words vault over words,
Truth is made bare,
Phenomena congeal.
There, falsehood, scattering light, takes on a shape.
A poem is the lens,
And the dark box a whirlpool of light.

11. ———: *Bird.* Polychrome impression, 10 × 8 in. Published in 1935. Carved, printed, and published by the artist. Edition: see note below. Blocks: 3 blocks of solid *katsura;* 3 printing stages. Pigment: poster colors. Paper: *torinoko.* Location: collection of the author. Notes: Onchi made this print to illustrate a book of his poems which was published in a limited edition of 50. For the book an artisan did the printing from Onchi's blocks, but Onchi printed a few extra copies, of which the author's is one.

12. ———: *Lyric Number 13: Melancholy of Japan.* Polychrome impression, 23 1/2 × 20 1/4 in. Published in 1952. Carved, printed, and published by the artist. Edition: 3. Blocks: 1 block of plywood faced with *buna* for the white background, and 9 blocks of various papers including *kozo,* waxed paper, and machine-made paper; 10 printing stages. Pigment: poster colors, *sumi,* and for the large triangular block in the middle, *shibu,* a sort of varnish containing persimmon juice and commonly used to coat Japanese paper umbrellas. Paper: *torinoko.* Location: collection of the author. Notes: Onchi made this print for the Salon du Printemps and an exhibition at the Art Institute of Chicago. It is one of a series of abstract designs which are numbered as "Lyrics."

13. ———: *Poem Number 8-1: Butterfly.* Polychrome impression, 14 7/8 × 13 in. Published in 1948. Carved, printed, and published by the artist. Edition: 10; since Onchi's death Koichi Hirai has been commissioned to print an indefinite number as a memorial edition. Blocks: 2 blocks of solid *katsura;* 8 printing stages. Pigment: poster color for the black block in the upper left corner; *sumi* for the wing of the butterfly which extends from that block; gouache for the leaf, the blue clouds lower right, and the grey area around the extended wing. Paper: *torinoko.* Location: Honolulu Academy of Arts and the collection of the author. Notes: There are two versions of this print, because Onchi recarved the clouds to make them slightly larger (the print reproduced is the original version). The leaf is a real leaf mounted on the block, and the grey area around the extended wing is printed from cloth fastened to the block. This is from the series of prints which Onchi called "Poems." He also wrote an accompanying poem, dated May 9, 1948, here translated:

The Butterfly

Now the wings are fully spread,
The black curtain falls into a space of
lines.
Yesterday it was shut inside its hard
husk,
But now
The butterfly goes heavenward to lay
its eggs.

14. ———: *Poem Number 22: Leaf and Clouds.* Polychrome impression, 17 3/4 × 13 1/2 in. Published in 1953. Carved, printed, and published by the artist. Edition: 10. Blocks: 4 blocks of waxed paper, 1 block made from a natural leaf; 10 printing stages. Pigment: *sumi* and water color. Paper: *kyokushi.* Location: collection of the author. Notes: This is one of the series of compositions numbered as "Poems." For a description of how this print was made, see text.

15. Un'ichi Hiratsuka: *At the Foot of Mt. Amagi.* Ink impression, 15 1/2 × 12 3/8 in. Published in 1954. Carved, printed, and published by the artist. Edition: indefinite (2 printed to date). Block: single block of solid *katsura;* I printing stage. Pigment: *sumi.* Paper: *hodomura.* Location: collection of the author. Notes: Mt. Amagi is more or less in the middle of the Izu peninsula. This view is from its south slopes. The artist states that he was interested in eliminating details and depicting masses shown against the light.

16. ———: *Nichiren Shonin.* Ink impression, 25 3/8 × 20 in. Published in 1931. Carved, printed, and published by the artist. Edition: indefinite (about 1,000 printed to date, see text). Block: single block of solid *katsura;* 1 printing stage (Hiratsuka states that it is an exceptionally good piece of *katsura,* and that, since very sharp lines are not essential in this print, he thinks he could get the 10,000 copies he would like to print). Pigment: *sumi.* Paper: two kinds have been used: when the artist makes a print to be mounted as a *kakemono* (hanging scroll) he uses a thin *kozo* paper made in Yamanashi and called *hosokawa;* when he makes a print to be framed he uses a stock of old

torinoko. Location: Honolulu Academy of Arts and the collection of the author. Notes: Nichiren (1222–1282) founded the Nichiren sect of Buddhism. Hiratsuka's family belonged to the Nichiren sect, and he says that he wanted to show the warm and kindly side of a man usually portrayed as stern or angry. Of the artist's prints, he has made most copies of this one, although more copies have been made of several prints commercially commissioned to be designed by him but printed by artisans.

17. ———: *Rakan Temple in the Rain.* Polychrome impression, 13 3/4 × 11 3/8 in. Published in 1935. Carved, printed, and published by the artist. Edition: indefinite (about 50 printed to date). Blocks: 6 blocks of solid *katsura;* 8 printing stages. Pigment: *sumi,* water colors, and Japanese pigment (blue). Paper: *hodomura.* Location: collection of the author. Notes: This temple, located in Kyushu's mountainous valley of Yabakei near Nakatsu City, used to be favored by poets and artists. Hiratsuka states that, since he wanted to capture the atmosphere of the Edo period (1615–1868), he used the technique of traditional *nishikie* (*ukiyoe* color prints).

18. ———: *Sutra Repository of Iwayadera.* Ink impression, 23 5/8 × 23 5/8 in. Published in 1940. Carved, printed, and published by the artist. Edition: indefinite (about 10 printed to date). Block: single block of solid *katsura;* 1 printing stage. Pigment: *sumi.* Paper: *hodomura.* Location: collection of the author. Notes: The Buddhist temple of Iwaya-dera, located in Aichi Prefecture near Nagoya, is noted for its complete collection of sutras printed in China by wood block during the Sung period. These sutras, called Sohan Issaikyo in Japan, are housed in the building shown in this print. Hiratsuka states that he was particularly attracted by the interesting construction under the roof.

19. ———: *Stone Buddhist Image.* Polychrome impression, 20 13/16 × 14 9/16 in. Published in 1946. Carved, printed, and published by the artist. Edition: indefinite (about 10 printed to date). Blocks:

2 blocks of solid *sakura,* 3 blocks of solid *katsura;* 5 printing stages. Pigment: *sumi* and Japanese pigments. Paper: *hodomura.* Location: collection of the author. Notes: The figure shown in this print is one of the 5th century sculptures in the caves at Yün-kang near Tatung in China. It is the right attendant of a group of three in the main room of the third cave, and is about 20 feet high. Hiratsuka sketched it during a trip to China in 1943.

20. ———: *Nandaimon.* Ink impression, 22 1/4 × 28 1/2 in. Published in 1937. Carved, printed, and published by the artist. Edition: indefinite (about 6 printed to date). Block: single block of solid *katsura;* 1 printing stage. Pigment: *sumi.* Paper: *hodomura.* Location: collection of the author. Notes: This is the great south gate to the city of Seoul, and is called Nam-tä-mun by the Koreans. Hiratsuka sketched it on the third of his four visits to Korea. In the absence of a tree or something similar in the foreground, he used the shadow of a nearly building to give distance, and balanced it in the background by a flight of some of the numerous crows which frequented the place.

21. ———: *The Innermost Temple of Koyasan.* Ink impression, 14 3/4 × 17 13/16 in. Published in 1941. Carved, printed and published by the artist. Edition: indefinite (about 10 printed to date). Block: single block of solid *katsura;* 1 printing stage. Pigment: *sumi.* Paper: *hodomura.* Location: collection of the author. Notes: This print shows the road leading to Okuno-in, the "Innermost Temple" on Mt. Koya, in Kii Prefecture. The temple, which can be seen through the trees in the middle, is dedicated to Kobo Daishi (774—835), the founder of the Shingon sect of Buddhism. The artist states that he was particularly impressed by the immensity of the old cryptomeria trees and by the old cemetery, lower left, with its graves of both lords and peasants.

22. Sempan Maekawa: *Kyoto Flower Vendor.* Polychrome impression, 14 1/2 × 11 3/8 inches. Published in 1951. Carved, printed, and published by the artist. Edition:

indefinite (about 20 printed to date). Blocks: 6 blocks of plywood faced with *shina;* 10 printing stages. Pigment: Japanese pigments for red and blue; poster colors for other colors. Paper: *torinoko.* Location: Art Institute of Chicago, Honolulu Academy of Arts, and the collection of the author. Notes: No model was used in designing this print. Maekawa says there are still vendors like this in Kyoto, but that there were more of them when he was a boy.

23. ———: *Factory District.* Polychrome impression, 9 7/16 × 13 7/8 in. Published in 1929. Carved, printed, and published by the artist. Edition: about 20 (the blocks have been destroyed). Blocks: 6 blocks of solid *katsura;* 6 printing stages. Pigment: poster colors and Japanese pigments. Paper: *torinoko.* Location: collection of the author. Notes: In this early print Maekawa was still using the curved-blade chisel. The place is Tokyo's factory district of Shibaura. Maekawa notes that this was a period when there was great public interest in construction and such pictures were a fad, but that in this case there was no political ideology at work.

24. ———: *An Inn at Kamisuwa.* Polychrome impression, 17 × 20 11/16 in. Published in 1932. Carved, printed, and published by the artist. Edition: 6 or 7 (the blocks have been destroyed). Blocks: 8 blocks of solid *katsura;* 8 printing stages. Pigment: poster colors and Japanese pigments. Paper: *torinoko.* Location: collection of the author. Notes: This print was made for an exhibition and is close to traditional *nishikie* (*ukiyoe* color prints) in composition and technique. Accordingly, the primary tool in cutting the blocks was a flat chisel with an angled blade. Kamisuwa is on the shores of Lake Suwa in the central, mountainous area of the main island of Honshu.

25. ———: *Cherry Festival.* Polychrome impression, 11 11/16 × 15 3/8 in. Published in 1941. Carved, printed, and published by the artist. Edition: 36 (the blocks have been destroyed). Blocks: 8 blocks of solid *katsura;* 8 printing stages. Pigment: poster colors. Paper: *torinoko.* Location: private

collection, Tokyo. Notes: The blocks for this print were cut primarily with flat chisels, both angled- and square-end. Mae-kawa published the print as one of six in a subscription series; only subscribers were able to get the print, and after completing the edition the blocks were destroyed. Maekawa lifted the design from the central portion of one of his earlier prints on the same subject (the older print is reproduced in Fujikake: *Japanese Wood-block Prints*). The place is Yukyuzan Park, Echigo Naga-oka, Niigata Prefecture.

26. ———: *A Spa*. Polychrome impression, 18 1/2 × 16 1/8 in. Published in 1949. Carved, printed, and published by the artist. Edition: 5 (Maekawa still has the essential line block, but the blocks for the flat, colored areas have been destroyed; however, these could be replaced without difficulty if he decides to make more prints). Blocks: 1 block of solid *katsura* (the line block which the artist still has), 3 blocks of plywood faced with *shina*; 4 printing stages. Pigment: poster colors. Paper: *torinoko*. Location: Museum of Fine Arts, Boston. Notes: The scene is a public bath at a spa in Beppu, Kyushu.

27. ———: *Plum Orchard*. Polychrome impression, 9 3/16 × 11 1/2 in. Published in 1943. Carved, printed, and published by the artist. Edition: indefinite (about 25 printed to date). Blocks: 4 blocks of solid *katsura*; 6 printing stages. Pigment: poster colors. Paper: *torinoko*. Location: collection of the author. Notes: The blocks for this print were carved with a square-end flat chisel, Maekawa's primary tool beginning with that period. The place is Yoshi-no, on the upper Tama River, near Tokyo.

28. ———: *Bird in Hand*. Polychrome impression, 11 5/16 × 16 9/16 in. Published in 1955. Carved, printed, and published by the artist. Edition: indefinite (10 printed to date). Blocks: 4 blocks of plywood faced with *shina*; 11 printing stages. Pigment: Japanese pigment for the red of the lips, cheek, and ribbon; poster colors for other colors. Paper: *torinoko*. Location: Hono-lulu Academy of Arts and the collection of the author. Notes: Maekawa notes that all affection is centered on the bird, and that everything else in the picture is simplified. He once had such a bird (a kind of titmouse which the Japanese call *yamagara*) and made sketches of it from which this print was made.

29. Kiyoshi Saito: *Staring*. Polychrome impression, 23 3/4 × 16 1/4 in. Published in 1950. Carved, printed, and published by the artist. Edition: 30 (exhausted). Blocks: 2 blocks of solid *katsura*; 4 printing stages; the blocks were carved by *kiri* except for the eye and small flowers on the face, where a knife was used. Pigment: *sumi* and gouache, with mica dusted on the white areas while they were still wet; when dry, Saito brushed the mica areas with a thin liquid glue. Paper: two kinds have been used: first prints were made on *obonai*, a *kozo* and pulp paper marked by prominent silky strands, which is made in Echizen, Fukui Prefecture; later prints have been made on *kizuki hosho*. Location: Museum of Fine Arts, Boston, and the collection of the author. Notes: This is the print which won the prize at the Sao Paulo Biennial (see text). Saito got the idea from sketching flowers.

30. ———: *Winter in Aizu*. Ink impression, 15 × 17 11/16 in. Published in 1941. Carved, printed, and published by the artist. Edition: indefinite (about 60 printed to date). Blocks: 2 blocks of plywood faced with *shina*; 2 printing stages. Pigment: *sumi*, watered to various shades of grey; shadings also obtained by the manner in which the ink is brushed on the block. Paper: *kizuki hosho*; early prints were made on a thin grade, but Saito now uses thick paper. Location: collection of the author. Notes: This print is one of a series of nostalgic prints picturing winter snow in Saito's home country of Aizu, Fukushima Prefecture.

31. ———: *Buddhist Statue*. Ink impression, with mica added, 19 3/4 × 11 1/4 in. Published in 1950. Carved, printed, and published by the artist. Edition: 50 (exhausted). Blocks: 2 blocks of solid *katsura*; 2 printing stages; the blocks were carved entirely by *kiri*; one block was used for the figure and one for the background. Pig-

ment: *sumi* and mica; the background block was used to apply only glue, on which mica was dusted. Paper: two kinds have been used: early prints were made on *torinoko*, later prints on *kizuki hosho*. Location: collection of the author. Notes: The artist sketched this statue from an Asuka period (552–645) bronze of Miroku Bosatsu in the National Museum, Ueno, Tokyo. Miroku Bosatsu (Sanskrit: Maitreya) is the Buddha of Compassion.

32. ———: *Naoko*. Polychrome impression, 9 × 8 3/16 in. Published in 1949. Carved, printed, and published by the artist. Edition: limited to 50 (about 25 printed to date). Blocks: 4 blocks of solid *katsura*; 7 printing stages. Pigment: *sumi* and gouache. Paper: *hodomura*. Location: collection of the author. Notes: This is a portrait of Saito's daughter and only child, sketched when she was five.

33. ———: *Shoji*. Polychrome impression, 10 3/4 × 27 7/8 in. Published in 1954. Carved, printed, and published by the artist. Edition: limited to 50 (about 40 printed to date). Blocks: 2 blocks of plywood faced with *shina*; 5 printing stages. Pigment: *sumi* and gouache. Paper: *hodomura*. Location: collection of the author. Notes: The design was suggested by the *shoji* (sliding paper-panel doors) of the Katsura Imperial Villa, Kyoto (see text).

34. ———: *Alone*. Polychrome impression, 22 × 17 in. Published in 1947. Carved, printed, and published by the artist. Edition: limited to 30 (8 printed to date). Block: single block of solid *katsura*; 6 printing stages. Pigment: on prints made to date, the artist has used tube water colors, but he states that from now on he will use gouache. Paper: a thick *hosho* paper from an old stock. Location: collection of the author. Notes: The design for this print was sketched from a model, a girl from Akita Prefecture whose features Saito found both pictorial and foreign looking. For a description of how this print was made, see text.

35. ———: *Earthenware and Haniwa*. Polychrome impression, 29 7/8 × 17 1/2 in.

Published in 1952. Carved, printed, and published by the artist. Edition: limited to 30 (11 printed to date). Blocks: 4 blocks of plywood faced with *rawan*; 5 printing stages. Pigment: gouache and mica, the mica being dusted on while the paint was still wet. Paper: to date Saito has used *obonai* (the same paper used originally for *Staring*), but he states that in the future he will use *kizuki hosho*. Location: collection of the author. Notes: The design was sketched from a *haniwa* in the National Museum, Ueno, Tokyo.

36. ———: *All Cats Are Grey at Night*. Polychrome impression, 23 3/4 × 17 3/4 in. Published in 1952. Carved, printed, and published by the artist. Edition: 40 (exhausted). Blocks: 4 blocks of plywood faced with *shina*; 4 printing stages. Pigment: *sumi* and gouache. Paper: two papers have been used: early prints were made on *obonai* (see notes concerning print 29), later prints on *kizuki hosho*. Location: collection of the author. Notes: Saito's model was his own black cat, sketched while staring up toward the rafters where mice were playing.

37. Jun'ichiro Sekino: *My Daughter*. Polychrome impression, 18 3/16 × 14 5/8 in. Published in 1952. Carved, printed, and published by the artist. Edition: limited to 30 (20 printed to date). Blocks: 5 blocks of plywood faced with *shina*; 12 printing stages. Pigment: French water colors for the earth colors; Japanese pigments for the red; ordinary water colors for the other colors; mica. Paper: a special *torinoko*, made in Echizen, Fukui Prefecture. Location: collection of the author. Notes: This is a portrait of Sekino's daughter, Ayuko, at the age of 5. The design was made in oil, traced onto the blocks with carbon paper.

38. ———: *Kichiemon, Kabuki Actor*. Polychrome impression, 21 3/4 × 17 3/4 in. Published in 1947. Carved, printed, and published by the artist. Edition: limited to 30 (about 25 printed to date). Blocks: 6 blocks of plywood faced with *shina*; 15 printing stages. Pigment: two types of *sumi*, ordinary black and a bluish kind; French water colors for the earth colors and

red; Japanese vegetable pigments for the other colors. Paper: *hosokawa* for early prints with three background figures, *torinoko* for later prints with one background figure. Location: Art Institute of Chicago; Museum of Fine Arts, Boston; Honolulu Academy of Arts; and the collection of the author. Notes: For the story of how Sekino came to make this portrait of Kichiemon I (1886–1954), see text. The first few copies of this print have one or two small background figures above Kichiemon's head, in addition to the figure at the side as shown in the copy reproduced here. The figure at the side is taken from Sharaku's portrait of Tomisaburo Segawa II as Yadorigi, wife of Kurando Ogishi, in the play *Hana-ayame Bunroku Soga* (The Iris Soga of the Bunroku Era) produced at the Miyako Theatre in 1794 (this Sharaku print is reproduced in Michener's book, and additional information about it is available there). The two smaller figures, not shown in the copy reproduced here, were taken from the cartoon sketches in two of Kuniyoshi's series of five prints called *Nitakara-gurakabe no Muda-gaki*, which may be roughly translated as *Doodlings on the Storeroom Walls*. The right figure is that of Kodanji Ichikawa IV in *O-Some Hisamatsu Ukina no Ukeuri* (The Rumored Love Affair of O-Some and Hisamatsu), as produced at the Ichimura Theatre in 1848; the left figure is that of Shuka Bando as Shizuka Gozen, in the play *Yoshitsune Sembon Zakura* (Yoshitsune and the Thousand Cherry Trees), also as produced at the Ichimura Theatre in 1848. None of the actors or the roles shown in the background figures has any special relationship to Kichiemon: Sekino introduced them simply to provide Kabuki atmosphere. Kichiemon is shown as a man, offstage, rather than as an actor on stage.

39. ——: *Aquarium*. Polychrome impression, 22 1/8 × 17 7/8 in. Published in 1947. Carved, printed, and published by the artist. Edition: 3. Blocks: 2 blocks of plywood faced with *shina;* 1 block of plywood faced with *buna* (used for the heavy grain effect at the top); 30 printing stages; the blocks were carved progressively for each new step of the printing, and so were automatically destroyed in making the

print (the original printing of 3 was therefore the total number of prints which could be made). The central black area was not made with a block but with a paper cutout laid over another paper heavily treated with printing ink, in which string had been laid; the paper being printed was then laid face down over the printing ink and printed in an etching press. Pigment: printing ink and Japanese tube water colors. Paper: *hosokawa,* a *kozo* paper made in Yamanashi. Location: collection of the author. Notes: Sekino was brought up near the sea and always liked to sketch fishes and shells. This composition resulted from accumulated sketches.

40. ——: *Eizo and Matsuomaru*. Polychrome impression, 19 × 24 7/8 in. Published in 1953. Carved, printed, and published by the artist. Edition: limited to 30 (29 printed to date). Blocks: 6 blocks of plywood faced with *shina,* 1 block of solid *katsura* (for facial details); 21 printing stages. Pigment: two types of *sumi,* ordinary black and a bluish kind; French water colors for the earth colors of the faces; Japanese pigments for red and blue; gouache for green, yellow, ochre, and light red; poster color for white; Japanese tube water colors for other colors. Paper: *torinoko.* Location: Art Institute of Chicago, Honolulu Academy of Arts, and the collection of the author. Notes: This is one of Sekino's studies of Japan's great puppet theatre, Bunraku. Shown here is Eizo Yoshida manipulating the puppet Matsuomaru in the scene called *Terakoya* (The Village School), which is part of a long play, *Sugawara Denju Tenarai Kagami* (The Lustrous Imparting of Sugawara's Calligraphic Secrets). The climactic moment shown is that in which Matsuomaru inspects the head of his own son, whom he has arranged to have sacrificed in order to save the son of his former lord, Sugawara; a minute later he will falsely certify that the head is that of Sugawara's son. The puppet whose head is shown behind Matsuomaru is Tonami, the wife of the schoolmaster. (For further discussion of the play see *Japanese Theater* by Faubion Bowers). Sekino did the sketches in the theatre during performances at the Shimbashi Embujo, Tokyo, in 1947.

41. ———: *Monjuro and Jihei*. Polychrome impression, 18 13/16 × 24 5/8 in. Published in 1954. Carved, printed, and published by the artist. Edition: limited to 30 (10 printed to date). Blocks: 6 blocks of plywood faced with *shina*, 1 block of plywood faced with *rawan*; 24 printing stages. Pigment: same as print 40. Paper: *torinoko*. Location: Museum of Fine Arts, Boston; Honolulu Academy of Arts; and the collection of the author. Notes: This print forms a pair with *Eizo and Matsuomaru* (print 40). The puppeteer at the left is Monjuro Kiritake manipulating the puppet Koharu. The puppeteer in the center holds O-Sui, daughter of Jihei. (The puppeteer was Monsho Kiritake but this is not a portrait of him.) At the right is the puppet Jihei, who is being manipulated by an unseen puppeteer. The scene is from Chikamatsu's play *Shinju Ten no Amijima* (Bridge to Heaven by the Suicide at Amijima), which is also discussed in Bower's *Japanese Theatre*. The scene is that in which a letter is read which O-San, Jihei's wife, has written on the kimono of her daughter, O-Sui. Sekino did the sketches for this print the same time as those for *Eizo and Matsuomaru*.

42. ———: *A Boy and His Rooster*. Polychrome impression, 24 × 17 7/8 in. Published in 1954. Carved, printed, and published by the artist. Edition: limited to 30 (12 printed to date). Blocks: 3 blocks of plywood faced with *shina*, 4 blocks of plywood faced with *rawan*; 21 printing stages. Pigment: *sumi* (the bluish type), French water colors for the earth colors, Japanese pigment for red, gouache for brown. Paper: *torinoko*. Location: collection of the author. Notes: The boy shown is Sekino's older boy, Jumpei, at the age of 12, with the rooster he had raised from a chick. The design was made in water color and was transferred to the blocks by means of mimeograph stencils.

43. ———: *My Son*. Polychrome impression, 18 1/4 × 14 5/8 in. Published in 1952. Carved, printed, and published by the artist. Edition: limited to 30 (20 printed to date). Blocks: 5 blocks of plywood faced with *shina*; 14 easily defined printing stages plus

several additional to achieve satisfactory flesh tones. The newspaper area at the left is printed as follows: newspapers are torn and arranged (since they can only be printed from once, the newspaper pattern is different in each print); soapy water, with a little cooking oil added, is brushed on the newspapers; a paper pattern with a cut-out area the size of that to be printed is placed over the newspapers; the picture is placed face down over the newspapers and the *baren* used with heavy pressure. Pigment: French water colors for the earth colors and red; Japanese pigments for the other colors; mica. Paper: a special *torinoko*, made in Echizen, Fukui Prefecture. Location: Art Institute of Chicago. Notes: This is a portrait of Sekino's second son, Yosaku, at the age of 8. The design was made in oil, traced onto the blocks with carbon paper.

44. Takumi Shinagawa: *Kabuki Actor*. Polychrome impression, 21 1/4 × 13 in. Published in 1953. Carved, printed, and published by the artist. Edition: indefinite (about 15 printed to date). Blocks: 5 blocks of plywood faced with *shina*; 5 printing stages. Pigment: German pigments, *gofun* (Japanese white), and mica. Paper: *torinoko*. Location: Art Institute of Chicago. Notes: The block with the grain pattern was cut with curved-blade chisels, other blocks were carved with flat chisels. Mica is added to the *gofun* used for the grain pattern and also to the black; powdered mica is put on the block with a spatula, after which the wet pigment is brushed onto the block and mixed with the mica. The design was suggested by the *kumadori* make-up used in certain Kabuki plays; this is one of a series of prints Shinagawa based on this idea. The print is not intended to suggest any particular role or actor.

45. ———: *Stone Buddha*. Polychrome impression, 19 3/4 × 22 5/8 in. Published in 1947. Carved, printed and published by the artist. Edition: indefinite (about 15 printed to date). Blocks: 4 blocks of plywood faced with *shina*; 4 printing stages. Pigment: German pigments (the same green is used throughout, lightened by different amounts of yellow). Paper: *torinoko* (at

the time the first prints were made, the available paper was so thin that Shinagawa pasted a thin sheet of another paper to the back; however, this is not necessary now). Location: Museum of Fine Arts, Boston, and the collection of the author. Notes: Shinagawa's idea was to portray the beauty of ruins. The head was sketched from a statue in his studio. Shinagawa thinks this is the only print for which he mixed his pigments before printing; his usual method, as explained in the text, is to mix colors in the paper by printing one over another.

46. ———: *Concaves*. Ink impression, 26 1/4×21 1/2 in. Published in 1951. Carved, printed, and published by the artist. Edition: indefinite (7 printed to date). Block: single block of plywood faced with *shina;* 4 printing stages (starting with the light grey, ending with the black). Pigment: *sumi,* chalk for the light greys and liquid for the dark grey and black. Paper: thin *torinoko,* supported by another paper pasted to the back. Location: collection of the artist. Notes: The title of the print is meant to suggest the sense of depth in the curves of the face. Shinagawa used no model, wanted to make a dynamic face like those of Greek terra-cotta figures or *haniwa.* The block was first carved with shallow curved chisels and then the contours were roughened with a wood file.

47. ———: *Cloud*. Polychrome impression, 29 × 20 1/2 in. Published in 1949. Carved, printed, and published by the artist. Edition: indefinite (7 printed to date). Block: single block of solid *katsura;* 1 printing stage. Pigment: a dry, powdered pigment, brown Bavarian conte-crayon. Paper: *torinoko.* Location: collection of the author. Notes: Since Shinagawa used dry, powdered pigment, the technique of this print is unusual. The powdered pigment is brushed onto the shallow-cut block with the shading tool of the type used in charcoal drawing, a pencil-like tool made of a roll of fine leather. The paper is sized and moistened, and the damp paper absorbs the dry pigment. So far as Shinagawa knows, this is an original technique and has been used by no one else. The idea for the design came from watching clouds.

48. ———: *Devil Tile*. Polychrome impression, 12 1/2×19 5/8 in. Published in 1954. Carved, printed, and published by the artist. Edition: indefinite (2 printed to date). Blocks: 4 blocks of plywood faced with *shina;* 4 printing stages. Pigment: German pigments mixed with water colors so they will seep into the paper deeply. Paper: *torinoko.* Location: collection of the author. Notes: The design was suggested by the tiles used at the end of a hip or ridge of a roof, called devil tiles because they were supposed to ward off devils. Shinagawa got the idea from a book of Chinese tiles, including a number of devil tiles. Technically, this print is one of several in which he attempts to get complicated color effects by superimposing primary colors. The grainy portion is carved with small curved-blade chisels in such a way that the colors printed below sometimes show through, and are sometimes overlayed with different combinations of the colors printed above.

49. ———: *Face on the Body*. Polychrome impression, 22 1/4×15 9/16 in. Published in 1952. Carved, printed, and published by the artist. Edition: indefinite (about 15 printed to date). Blocks: 4 blocks of plywood faced with *shina,* 1 block of plywood faced with *rawan* (the dark, heavily grained portion in the middle), 1 block of plywood faced with crumpled rice paper; 6 printing stages. Pigment: water colors, and (for the dark portion made with the *rawan* block) water color thickened with a little oil paint called easel paint. Paper: *torinoko.* Location: collection of the author. Notes: The block faced with paper is the ground block which underlies the entire print, and, printed in yellow, gives the irregular pattern inside the frame on both sides of the dark middle portion. In using the *rawan* block Shinagawa emphasizes the grain by brushing the color sideways so that the pigment accumulates against the grain. Shinagawa's idea in designing the print was that, while people usually remember a person by his face, the body has its equally distinctive characteristics.

50. ———: *Ghost Story*. Polychrome impression, 31×22 1/4 in. Published in 1955.

Carved, printed, and published by the artist. Edition: indefinite (4 printed to date). Blocks: 10 blocks of plywood faced with *shina;* 16 printing stages. Pigment: German pigments mixed with water colors so they will seep into the paper. Paper: *torinoko.* Location: collection of the artist. Notes: Technically, this is another of Shinagawa's experiments in attaining complicated color effects by overlaying colors. The blocks are carved chiefly with small curved-blade chisels in such a way that the colors printed below sometimes show through, and are sometimes overlayed with different combinations of the colors printed above. Shinagawa got the idea for his design from his children, scared of being alone at night after hearing a ghost story. The combination of their fright and their avid interest brought back memories of his own childhood.

51. Shiko Munakata: *Ragora.* Ink impression, 40 1/2 × 16 in. Published in 1937. Carved, printed, and published by the artist. Edition: indefinite (about 30 printed to date). Block: single block of solid *katsura;* 1 printing stage. Pigment: *sumi.* Paper: *izumo.* Location: collection of the author. Notes: This print of Ragora (Sanskrit: Râhula) is from Munakata's series *The Ten Great Disciples of Buddha,* and with two other figures from the series won him the *hanga* prize at Sao Paulo's 1955 international show.

52.———: *The Deity of the Wind.* Ink impression, 11 3/4 × 15 1/4 in. Published in 1937. Carved, printed, and published by the artist. Edition: about 30 (the blocks were destroyed during the war). Block: single block of solid *katsura;* 1 printing stage. Pigment: *sumi.* Paper: *izumo.* Location: Folk Art Museum (Mingei-kan), Tokyo. Notes: This print is from the *Kegon Series* (see text).

53. ———: *Magora.* Ink impression with color added, 16 1/2 × 20 7/8 in. Published in 1938. Carved, printed, and published by the artist. Edition: between 5 and 10 (the blocks were destroyed during the war). Block: single block of solid *katsura;* 1 printing stage. Pigment: *sumi,* with brown water color brushed on the back of the print.

Paper: *izumo.* Location: Folk Art Museum (Mingei-kan), Tokyo. Notes: This print is from *Illustrations to the Kannon Sutra,* a series which shows the 33 manifestations of the Kannon (with the title print and end print, the series consists of 35 pictures). The manifestations start at the top with Buddha; and Magora (Sanskrit: Maharaga), a guardian demi-god, is the 32nd, next to the bottom.

54. ———: *The Garden.* Ink impression, 15 1/4 × 14 1/2 in. Published in 1950. Carved, printed, and published by the artist. Edition: indefinite (13 printed to date). Block: single block of solid *katsura;* 1 printing stage. Pigment: *sumi.* Paper: *etchu.* Location: Honolulu Academy of Arts and the collection of the author. Notes: This garden was suggested by the garden of a house Munakata once lived in. It is inhabited by *kappa,* the legendary water creatures of Japan, who are enormously powerful as long as the hollow on top of their head is filled with water.

55. ———: *Hawk Woman.* Ink impression, 16 1/16 × 12 5/16 in. Published in 1955. Carved, printed, and published by the artist. Edition: indefinite (4 printed to date). Block: single block of solid *katsura;* 1 printing stage. Pigment: *sumi.* Paper: *izumo.* Location: Honolulu Academy of Arts and the collection of the author. Notes: The title of the print is shown in the lower right corner, and the date (8 February 955—meant to be 1955) in the upper right corner. This is the first print to show Munakata's recent tendency toward sharp lines made with a V-shaped chisel.

56. ———: *Sand Nest.* Ink impression, 9 × 11 1/8 in. Published in 1938. Carved, printed, and published by the artist. Edition: indefinite (about 20 printed to date). Block: single block of solid *katsura;* 1 printing stage. Pigment: *sumi.* Paper: *izumo.* Location: Honolulu Academy of Arts and the collection of the author. Notes: This is one of a series of 30 prints based on the Noh drama, *Uto.* The *uto* are sea birds which make their nests in the sand of the beaches. According to legend, if

hunters find a nest and take the young birds the parent birds weep tears of blood, the touch of which causes sickness and death. The drama is the tragedy of an ill-fated hunter who is pursued in Hades by the birds he killed on earth.

57. ———: *Hisatsu*. Ink impression, 15 3/4 × 11 11/16 in. Published in 1954. Carved, printed, and published by the artist. Edition: indefinite (7 printed to date). Block: single block of solid *katsura;* 1 printing stage. Pigment: *sumi.* Paper: *izumo.* Location: collection of the author. Notes: This print is of the period when Munakata started to use dots for accents; carving is by curved chisel. Munakata explains that this print shows two female nudes, but that the upper signifies masculinity and the lower, femininity. In further contrast, the upper figure has a closed mouth signifying repose, and the lower figure has an open mouth signifying action.

58. Shigeru Hatsuyama: *Flowers, Birds.* Polychrome impression, 20 × 16 in. Published in 1953. Carved, printed, and published by the artist. Edition: 10. Block: single block of solid *katsura,* carved progressively for each new stage of the printing; 16 printing stages. Pigment: *ai* (blue vegetable pigment) and cobalt for the blues (the two pigments were not mixed but were blended by alternate printings), powdered mineral pigments for the rest. Paper: *ogawa,* a remade paper similar to *hodomura.* Location: Art Institute of Chicago. Notes: This print, subtitled *Bathing Beauties* by its admirers, is a modern interpretation of the traditional flower and bird subjects of *ukiyoe;* the figures represent flowers.

59. Sumio Kawakami: *Arrival of a Portuguese Ship.* Ink impression colored by hand, 15 1/4 × 24 3/4 in. Published in 1952. Carved, printed, hand-colored, and published by the artist. Edition: indefinite (about 15 printed to date). Blocks: 2 blocks of solid *katsura* (one block for the right grouping and one for the left); 2 printing stages. Pigment: the blocks are printed with *sumi* mixed with a little animal glue; Japanese water colors are brushed on. Paper:

torinoko. Location: collection of the author. Notes: The place is Nagasaki, the time about 400 years ago, the motif from Kawakami's imagination. The title of the print is given in the medallion.

60. ———: *Nambanesque Behavior*. Ink impression colored by hand, 16 1/4 × 21 1/2 in. Published in 1955. Carved, printed, hand-colored, and published by the artist. Edition: indefinite (15 printed to date). Block: single block of plywood faced with *shina;* 1 printing stage. Pigment: the block is printed with *sumi* mixed with a little animal glue; Japanese water colors are brushed on. Paper: a *kozo* paper from Tottori Prefecture, dyed in Tokyo, and commonly referred to as *somegami* (dyed paper); the artist has made this print on both yellow and brown papers. Location: collection of the author. Notes: This print was suggested by an old illustration. "Nambanesque" can be taken as meaning European or Western, and the title derives from the fact that in the period pictured, about 400 years ago, both beds and tobacco had just been introduced to Japan.

61. Takeo Takei: *Devils*. Polychrome impression 11 3/4 × 18 3/8 in. Published in 1952. Carved, printed, and published by the artist. Edition: 10. Blocks: 1 block of plywood faced with *rawan,* 4 blocks of plywood faced with *shina,* 1 paper block; 11 printing stages. Pigment: regular *sumi* for the grey of the border, special quality *sumi* for the black in the figures, poster colors for the rest. Paper: *masa hosho* (*kozo* and pulp). Location: collection of the author. Notes: Takei emphasizes that these are pet devils, not wicked ones, mischievous rather than evil. The border is printed from the *rawan* block, scoured with a stiff wire brush to accentuate the grain, and with the inner edge tapered to give a soft effect. The form in the face of the right-hand devil is made with the paper block, using Takei's "vari-type" technique (see text). String is glued to the block for the arms of the left-hand devil.

62. ———: *Landscape*. Polychrome impression, 13 3/4 × 19 5/8 in. Published in

1952. Carved, printed, and published by the artist. Edition: 6. Blocks: 5 blocks of plywood faced with *shina*, 3 paper blocks; 9 printing stages. Pigment: both regular and special-quality *sumi*, and poster colors. Paper: *masa hosho* (*kozo* and pulp). Location: collection of the author. Notes: The figure in the cage, the fish in the pool of blue beneath it, and the oval forms upper right are made with paper blocks using Takei's "vari-type" technique (see text); the three ovals are made by shifting one block.

63. Shigeru Hatsuyama: *The White Horse.* Polychrome impression, 9 1/2 × 13 in. Published in 1948. Carved, printed, and published by the artist. Edition: 20. Block: single block of solid *katsura*, carved progressively for each new stage of the printing; 14 printing stages. Pigment: *ai* and Japanese water colors. Paper: *ogawa*. Location: collection of the author. Notes: Hatsuyama is aware that a horse rarely walks as shown in this dreamlike print, but he says that when he sketched it walking normally (both legs on one side forward, both legs on the other side back) the animal always looked as though it were about to topple over.

64. ———: *Japanese Lanterns.* Polychrome impression, 14 3/4 × 17 3/4 in. Published in 1952. Carved, printed, and published by the artist. Edition: 10 (8 signed and numbered for sale and 2 for himself). Blocks: 1 block of solid *katsura* (for the plant), 1 block of plywood faced with *shina* (for the hands and linear background form), both carved progressively for each new stage of the printing; the *katsura* block was carved and printed in 33 different stages, the *shina* block in 4, including one for the signature—a total of 37 stages. Pigment: *ai, sumi,* and mineral powdered pigments. Paper: *torinoko* for the 8 prints made for sale, *ogawa* for the 2 for himself. Location: collection of the author. Notes: The design was suggested to Hatsuyama during a walk as he watched his daughter gather these flowers, which in Japan are called *hozuki*.

65. Hide Kawanishi: *Snow at the Lakeside.* Polychrome impression, 23 3/8 × 17

7/8 in. Published in 1942. Carved, printed, and published by the artist. Edition: indefinite (about 15 printed to date). Blocks: 4 blocks of solid *katsura*; 6 printing stages. Pigment: poster colors and *sumi.* Paper: *hodomura.* Location: collection of the author. Notes: The scene is along the coast of Honshu west of Kobe, near Mt. Taisen. In actuality the lake is on the other side of the mountains shown in the background, but Kawanishi moved it over for the sake of composition.

66. Tokushi Katsuhira: *Hearth.* Polychrome impression, 10 3/4 × 14 7/8 in. Published in 1939. Carved, printed, and published by artist. Edition: about 70. Blocks: 6 blocks of solid *ho;* 13 printing stages. Pigment: *sumi* and Japanese water colors. Paper: *hosho.* Location: collection of the author. Notes: This print is from the series *Ten Views of Akita Customs.*

67. ———: *Seller of Bonden.* Polychrome impression, 14 7/8 × 10 5/8 in. Published in 1935. Carved, printed, and published by the artist. Edition: about 40. Blocks: 6 blocks of solid *ho;* 8 printing stages. Pigment: *sumi* and Japanese water colors. Paper: *hosho.* Location: collection of the author. Notes: *Bonden,* sold during the New Year's season, are things dedicated to the gods. Another print from the series *Ten Views of Akita Customs.*

68. Susumu Yamaguchi: *Taisho-ike.* Polychrome impression, 17 × 22 3/4 in. Published in 1952. Carved, printed, and published by the artist. Edition: indefinite (20 printed to date). Blocks: 8 blocks of solid *katsura;* 14 printing stages. Pigment: powdered Japanese pigments, poster colors, and *sumi.* Paper: *torinoko;* an old stock of high quality. Location: collection of the author. Notes: This is one of Yamaguchi's prints of the volcano-formed lake at Kamikochi, Nagano Prefecture (see text).

69. ———: *Mt. Hodaka at Daybreak.* Polychrome impression, 13 1/4 × 19 1/2 in. Published in 1955. Carved, printed, and published by the artist. Edition: indefinite (3 printed to date). Blocks: 6 blocks of solid *katsura,* 1 block of plywood faced

with *katsura;* 9 printing stages. Pigment: powdered Japanese pigments, tube water colors, poster colors, and *sumi.* Paper: *kyokushi.* Location: collection of the author. Notes: Mt. Hodaka, over 10,000 feet high, is one of the principal peaks of the northern range of the Japan Alps.

70. Hide Kawanishi: *Iris Season.* Polychrome impression, 19×13 in. Published in 1955. Carved, printed, and published by the artist. Edition: indefinite (4 printed to date). Blocks: 3 blocks of solid *katsura;* 4 printing stages. Pigment: poster colors and *sumi.* Paper: *hodomura.* Location: collection of the author. Notes: This is a view of the garden of the Katsura Imperial Villa, Kyoto.

71. ———: *Interior with Narcissus.* Polychrome impression, 17 3/4×23 1/2 in. Published in 1947. Carved, printed, and published by the artist. Edition: indefinite (5 printed to date). Blocks: 4 blocks of solid *katsura;* 5 printing stages. Pigment: poster colors and *sumi.* Paper: *hodomura.* Location: collection of the artist. Notes: This print is a glimpse into the home of Kawanishi's son.

72. Tomikichiro Tokuriki: *Woman Combing Her Hair.* Polychrome impression, 13 3/4×9 1/2 in. Published in 1947. Carved, printed, and published by the artist. Edition: limited to 50 (30 printed to date). Blocks: 1 block of solid *sakura* (the line block), 4 blocks of solid *ho* (color areas); 10 printing stages. Pigment: Japanese powdered mineral pigments and *sumi.* Paper: *hosho* from Echizen. Location: Museum of Fine Arts, Boston, and collection of the author. Notes: This is a study of Tokuriki's wife.

73. ———: *Sanjo Bridge.* Polychrome impression, 14 3/8×19 1/2 in. Published in 1954. Carved, printed, and published by the artist. Edition: limited to 50 (10 printed to date). Blocks: 8 blocks of solid *ho;* 8 printing stages. Pigment: Japanese powdered mineral pigments and *sumi.* Paper: *hosho* from Echizen. Location: collection of the author. Notes: This is Kyoto's famous Sanjo Bridge, looking

downstream at evening-time, one of a series of creative prints Tokuriki plans on scenes around Kyoto.

74. Umetaro Azechi: *Staring at the Snow and Ice.* Polychrome impression, 20 7/8× 14 7/8 in. Published in 1953. Carved, printed, and published by the artist. Edition: limited to 10 (9 printed to date). Blocks: 6 blocks of plywood faced with *shina;* 15 printing stages. Pigment: Japanese tube water colors for the sky, lips, gloves, and the under-color of the rope; poster colors for the other areas. Paper: white *torinoko.* Location: collection of the author. Notes: Azechi used no model for this print, based it on composite impressions of mountaineers.

75. Kihachiro Shimozawa. *By the Window.* Polychrome impression, 19×22 5/8 in. Published in 1954. Carved, printed, and published by the artist. Edition: indefinite (5 printed to date). Blocks: 4 blocks of plywood faced with *shina;* 8 printing stages. Pigment: *sumi* and poster colors. Paper: *torinoko.* Location: collection of the author. Notes: Against the background of a window, this print shows a *haniwa,* an ancient burial figure from about 400 A.D., with a jar of the same age, and, partly out of the picture at the left, a jar of the Tempyo period (710 —794).

76. ———: *Ikari-ga-Seki.* Polychrome impression, 9 1/4×13 1/8 in. Published in 1949. Carved, printed, and published by the artist. Edition: indefinite (30 printed to date). Blocks: 1 block of solid *sakura,* 5 blocks of solid *ho,* 1 block of plywood faced with *shina;* 13 printing stages. Pigment: *sumi, ai* (Japanese blue vegetable pigment), and poster colors. Paper: *hosho.* Location: collection of the author. Notes: This print shows the village of Ikari-ga-Seki on the Hira River, with Mt. Ajara, a popular skiing ground, in the background; the place is in Aomori Prefecture, near the border of Akita Prefecture.

77. Masao Maeda: *Big Haul Net.* Polychrome impression, 23 1/2×31 1/4 in. Published in 1941. Carved, printed, and published by the artist. Edition: will probably

be limited to 10 (2 printed to date). Blocks: 8 blocks of plywood faced with *shina;* 20 printing stages. Pigment: Japanese powdered pigments mixed with thinly diluted animal glue. Paper: *torinoko.* Location: collection of the author. Notes: The scene is a beach at Ito on the Izu peninsula.

78. ———: *Black Cat.* Polychrome impression, 14 7/8 × 17 3/4 in. Published in 1940. Carved, printed, and published by the artist. Edition: limited to 50 (10 printed to date). Blocks: 7 blocks of plywood faced with *shina;* 7 printing stages. Pigment: water colors. Paper: *torinoko.* Location: collection of the author. Notes: Maeda sketched this scene when he saw his neighbor's cat in a pine tree.

79. Okiie Hashimoto: *Young Woman and Iris.* Polychrome impression, 15 3/8 × 21 3/8 in. Published in 1952. Carved, printed, and published by the artist. Edition: limited to 50 (16 printed to date). Blocks: 3 blocks of plywood faced with *shina;* 6 printing stages. Pigment: Japanese *ai* (blue vegetable pigment) for the blouse and skirt; *ai* mixed with *sumi* for the iris leaves; *sumi* for the hair; Japanese tube water colors for the rest. Paper: *torinoko.* Location: Honolulu Academy of Arts and the collection of the author. Notes: Hashimoto used a model for his sketch. The scene is the Shobu-en iris garden at Hodogaya in Yokohama. The gradation of tone in the hair is achieved by the way color is brushed on the block. In certain areas, like the lower right corner, the artist used his thumb as well as the *baren* to push the paper down into the carved areas and get an impression there. The blouse and leaves were carved with a curved-blade chisel, the flowers with a flat, straight-edged chisel.

80. ———: *Castle in Autumn.* Polychrome impression, 15 1/2 × 21 3/8 in. Published in 1954. Carved, printed, and published by the artist. Edition: limited to 50 (10 printed to date). Blocks: 7 blocks of plywood faced with *shina;* 15 printing stages. Pigment: *sumi, gofun* (Japanese white pigment), and Japanese tube water colors. Paper: *torinoko.* Location: Museum of Fine Arts, Boston; Honolulu Academy of Arts; and the collection of the author. Notes: The castle is Nishi-no-Maru, near Himeji, associated with the fabulous princess of Japanese history, Senhime (1597—1666).

81. Umetaro Azechi: *Mountaineer.* Polychrome impression, 16 1/4 × 11 3/8 in. Published in 1953. Carved, printed, and published by the artist. Edition: limited to 50 (26 printed to date). Blocks: 5 blocks of plywood faced with *shina;* 9 printing stages. Pigment: poster color for the black background, water colors for the rest. Paper: *torinoko.* Location: collection of the author. Notes: This print, like *Staring at the Snow and Ice,* is based on composite impressions of mountaineers.

82. ———: *Remains of a Volcano.* Polychrome impression, 11 1/4 × 16 1/4 in. Published in 1952. Carved, printed, and published by the artist. Edition: limited to 50 (about 30 printed to date). Blocks: 6 blocks of plywood faced with *shina;* 9 printing stages. Pigment: Japanese tube water colors for the sky and the red of the volcano, poster colors for the other areas. Paper: white *torinoko.* Location: collection of the author. Notes: Shown in this print is the active crater near the summit of Takachiho Peak, in Kirishima National Park on the island of Kyushu. This area is called Hyuga, and is celebrated as the birthplace of the Emperor Jimmu, supposed to have founded the Empire of Japan in 660 B.C.

83. Gen Yamaguchi: *Poetry of Early Autumn.* Polychrome impression, 11 1/2 × 11 1/2 in. Published in 1947. Carved (prepared), printed, and published by the artist. Edition: 7. Blocks: 20 blocks of natural leaves, 3 stencils; 23 printing stages. Pigment: poster colors. Paper: *torinoko.* Location: collection of the author. Notes: Yamaguchi made a *kento* on a piece of cardboard which bore pencil outlines to show the position for each leaf. Each leaf was placed separately on the cardboard and printed individually. Some were printed face up and others face down to vary the design made by the veins. The check mark and the two circles were made with stencils cut out of stiff paper; after the undercolor was brushed on through the stencil, another

color was printed on top, using leaves as blocks.

84. Masaji Yoshida: *Silence Number 50: Parting.* Polychrome impression, 5 7/8 × 14 3/4 in. Published in 1953. Cut, printed, and published by the artist. Edition: limited to 20 (4 printed to date). Blocks: "cut-out blocks" (see text) of solid *katsura,* 8 sections plus 2 plastic strips; 3 printing stages. Pigment: Japanese tube and ordinary water colors. Paper: *torinoko.* Location: collection of the author. Notes: Yoshida uses no *kento* when working with "cut-out blocks"; he tacks his paper to the edge of the frame. This is one of his prints in black, white, and tones of grey.

85. ———: *Fountain of Earth: Number 1.* Ink impression, 22 1/4 × 32 1/4 in. Published in 1956. Carved, printed, and published by the artist. Edition: limited to 50 (2 printed to date). Block: 1 block of plywood faced with *shina;* 1 printing stage. Pigment: a mixture of liquid *sumi* and black water color. Paper: *torinoko.* Location: collection of the artist. Notes: The theme of this print is growth and development. Yoshida plans a series of five prints based on this idea.

86. Fumio Kitaoka: *Ships at Rest.* Ink impression, 20 × 27 1/4 in. Published in 1952. Carved, printed, and published by the artist. Edition: limited to 20 (7 printed to date). Block: single block of plywood faced with *shina;* 1 printing stage. Pigment: *sumi.* Paper: *torinoko.* Location: collection of the author.

87. ———: *Still Life on a Table.* Polychrome impression, 14 × 17 3/4 in. Published in 1948. Carved, printed, and published by the artist. Edition: limited to 50 (20 printed to date). Blocks: 6 blocks of plywood faced with *shina;* 12 printing stages. Pigment: Japanese powdered pigments. Paper: *torinoko.* Location: collection of the author.

88. Gen Yamaguchi: *Window.* Polychrome impression, 14 1/2 × 10 7/8 in. Published in 1948. Carved, printed, and published by the artist. Edition: 10. Blocks: 2 blocks of unplaned *sugi* (cedar), 2 blocks of plywood faced with *shina,* 1 stencil; 5 printing stages. Pigment: poster colors. Paper: *masagami,* a *kozo* paper. Location: collection of the author. Notes: Yamaguchi's design developed from an urge to use rough, unplaned boards as blocks. Two such blocks form the background of this print, while the lines which outline the window are cut in plywood. The solid blue in the upper part of the window was applied using a stencil, and the circular form was printed in two stages, the color on top being printed from a block faced with a piece of net.

89. ———: *Human Beings.* Polychrome impression, 17 3/4 × 14 1/2 in. Published in 1953. Carved, printed, and published by the artist. Edition: 3. Blocks: 1 block of plywood faced with *shina,* 1 uncarved block of solid *katsura* on which paper blocks for the faces had been pasted, 5 blocks of plain cardboard, 2 blocks of corrugated cardboard; 9 printing stages. Pigment: poster colors. Paper: *masagami.* Location: collection of the author. Notes: The human beings portrayed are a man and woman of no particular race or country. In making the print, the background and faces were printed from the uncarved block of solid *katsura,* on which were pasted the face blocks of wrapping paper. Thinly diluted grey color was brushed over the entire block, but the paper repelled the color and printed much whiter. The noses, mouths, and eyes were carved on the plywood, the bodies were printed from the five blocks of plain cardboard, and the lines around the heads were printed from corrugated cardboard.

90. Tomoo Inagaki: *Cat Making Up.* Polychrome impression, 23 1/4 × 17 in. Published in 1955. Carved, printed, and published by the artist. Edition: limited to 30 (2 printed to date). Blocks: 4 blocks of plywood faced with *shina;* 12 printing stages. Pigment: water colors, and, for the black, *sumi* mixed with water color. Paper: white *torinoko.* Location: collection of the author. Notes: There is only one cat in this picture—Inagaki used the two positions of the head to form a dynamic composition of a cat washing itself.

91. ———: *Lamp.* Polychrome impres-

sion, 20 7/8 × 16 in. Published in 1954. Carved, printed, and published by the artist. Edition: limited to 30 (2 printed to date). Blocks: 4 blocks of plywood faced with *shina;* 9 printing stages. Pigment: poster colors, water colors, and, for the black, *sumi* mixed with water color. Paper: Echizen *hodomura.* Location: collection of the author. Notes: For this composition Inagaki used a persimmon from his yard and an oil lamp which saw service during the war when the electricity failed.

92. ———: *Record of My Crop.* Polychrome impression, 18 × 23 1/2 in. Published in 1949. Carved, printed, and published by the artist. Edition: limited to 20 (9 printed to date). Blocks: 5 blocks of plywood faced with *shina;* 12 printing stages. Pigment: Japanese tube water colors, poster colors, and, for the black, *sumi* mixed with water color. Paper: Echizen *hodomura.* Location: collection of the author. Notes: During the war people turned their yards into vegetable gardens; this print is the record of one of Inagaki's wartime crops and is from a sketch made in 1945. The original print was made from a block carved progressively with each new step of the printing. Later, when he wanted to make more prints, Inagaki carved new blocks for each of the steps prior to the final one, for which he uses the original block. This print has also been published in a somewhat smaller version for distribution by the International Graphic Arts Society.

93. Kihei Sasajima: *Early Winter in the Mountains.* Ink impression, 15 1/4 × 19 1/2 in. Published in 1947. Carved, printed, and published by the artist. Edition: indefinite (20 printed to date). Block: single block of solid *katsura;* 1 printing stage. Pigment: *sumi.* Paper: *torinoko.* Location: collection of the author. Notes: This print is a view of Mt. Asama from the heights of Kusatsu.

94. ———: *A Mountain Stream.* Ink impression, 18 × 23 5/8 in. Published in 1954. Carved, printed, and published by the artist. Edition: limited to 30 (2 printed to date). Block: single block of plywood faced with *shina;* 1 printing stage. Pig-

ment: *sumi.* Paper: *hosokawa,* a *kozo* paper. Location: collection of the author. Notes: This is a view near Otsushio hot spring in Aizu.

95. Toshi Yoshida: *Indian Village, New Mexico.* Polychrome impression, 10 3/4 × 19 1/2 in. Published in 1955. Carved, printed, and published by the artist. Edition: indefinite (about 40 printed to date). Blocks: 4 blocks of plywood faced with *shina;* 7 printing stages. Pigment: Japanese powdered pigments and *sumi.* Paper: *kizuki hosho.* Location: collection of the author. Notes: This print was made from sketches made at Taos in 1953.

96. Fujio Yoshida: *Myoga.* Polychrome impression, 14 3/4 × 9 3/4 in. Published in 1954. Carved, printed, and published by the artist. Edition: indefinite (about 30 printed to date). Blocks: 8 blocks of plywood faced with *shina;* 13 printing stages. Pigment: Japanese powdered pigments. Paper: *kizuki hosho.* Location: collection of the author. Notes: Myoga is a tiny flower in the ginger family, used as a flavoring for soups, salads, and *sashimi* (raw fish).

97. Hodaka Yoshida: *Buddhist Statues.* Polychrome impression, 14 3/4 × 9 3/4 in. Published in 1954. Carved, printed, and published by the artist. Edition: indefinite (about 30 printed to date). Blocks: 4 blocks of plywood faced with *shina,* 1 block of plywood faced with *rawan;* 7 printing stages. Pigment: tube water colors, powdered pigments, and *sumi.* Paper: *kizuki hosho.* Location: collection of the author. Notes: This print was made from sketches of various statues of the Buddhist deity Kannon in the temple called Kakurin-ji in Hyogo.

98. Chizuko Yoshida: *Frozen.* Polychrome impression, 9 3/4 × 14 3/8 in. Published in 1955. Carved, printed, and published by the artist. Edition: indefinite (about 20 printed to date). Blocks: 4 blocks of plywood faced with *shina;* 6 printing stages. Pigment: powdered pigments and tube water colors. Paper: *kizuki hosho.* Location: collection of the author. Notes: This print was made from numerous sketches of ice in different conditions.

99. Thoru Mabuchi: *Mountain Lake*. Polychrome impression, 10 1/2 × 16 5/8 in. Published in 1954. Carved, printed, and published by the artist. Edition: 50 (exhausted). Blocks: 1 uncarved block of plywood faced with *shina* for the ground color (ochre), 8 blocks of plywood faced with *rawan;* 20 printing stages. Pigment: poster colors and tube water colors. Paper: *hosho*. Location: collection of the author. Notes: Based on an oil sketch of Kido Pond at Shiga Heights, popular summer and winter resort in the Joshin'etsu National Park. This print was published for subscription sale.

100. ———: *Afternoon Sun*. Polychrome impression, 20 1/2 × 29 5/8 in. Published in 1953. Carved, printed, and published by the artist. Edition: 5. Blocks: 1 uncarved block of plywood faced with *shina* for the ground color (ochre), 2 carved blocks of plywood faced with *shina,* 7 mosaic blocks (see text); 30 printing stages. Pigment: poster colors and tube water colors. Paper: *ogawa,* a *kozo* paper. Location: Honolulu Academy of Arts. Notes: This print, an example of Mabuchi's mosaic technique, is based on an oil sketch of an old foundry in Kawasaki, near Tokyo, a subject which Mabuchi has used many times.

INDEX

(Note: Figures in italics refer to the numbered descriptions of prints given in Appendix 2; all other figures refer to page numbers.)